The Eucharist

Heart of the Christian Unity

Hegumen Abraam Sleman

The Eucharist: Heart of the Christian Unity

© January 2026, Hegumen Abraam D. Sleman

E-Mail: FrSleman@CopticChurch.net

All rights reserved. No part of this publication may be reproduced, stored in a retrieval system, or transmitted in any form or by any means: electronic, mechanical, photocopying, recording, or otherwise, without the prior written permission of the publisher, except in the case of brief quotations embodied in critical articles and reviews.

Second Edition Published January, 2026

ISBN: 978-1-971426-02-0

Unless otherwise indicated, Scripture quotations are from the Legacy Standard Bible (LSB), copyright © 2021 by The Lockman Foundation. All rights reserved. Used by permission. For additional information about the LSB, visit https://www.lockman.org

For other books published by Hegumen Abraam Sleman, please visit www.amazon.com/author/frsleman , frsleman.org, and frsleman.net

Table of Contents

Dedication 6
Preface 7
Introduction 9
Chapter 1 11
   Eucharist's Foreshadows in the Old Testament 11
Chapter 2 24
   Institution of the Eucharist 24
Chapter 3 38
   Eucharist and the One Body of Christ 38
Chapter 4 55
   Eucharist as a Unifying Reality in the Early Church 55
Chapter 5 75
   Historical Schisms and the Church Unity 75
Chapter 6 99
   The Tragedy of Eucharistic Separation 99
Chapter 7 119
   Eucharistic Unity: A Biblical Mandate 119
Chapter 8 140
   A Renewed Eucharistic Theology for Unity 140
Chapter 9 162
   Challenges to Eucharistic Unity 162
Chapter 10 187
   An Invitation to the Lord's Table 187
Chapter 11 214

The Marriage Supper of the Lamb 214
Conclusion 237
  The Eucharist as the Heart of Christian Unity 237
Epilogue 247
  A Personal Word from the Author 247
Bibliography 250

Dedication

To His Holiness Pope Tawadros II, Pope of Alexandria and Patriarch of the See of Saint Mark, with deepest love, respect, and gratitude for Your Holiness' fatherly heart, your steadfast love for the Church, and your gracious, welcoming spirit that embraces all with wisdom, humility, and hope.

May God continue to strengthen Your Holiness as a shepherd of unity, guiding Christ's flock with the love of the Father, the grace of the Son, and the fellowship of the Holy Spirit.

Preface

This book was born out of a deep longing that has shaped my heart for many years: the longing to see the Church of Christ truly united, not only in word or aspiration but in lived communion. I have watched with sorrow as well-meaning efforts for Christian unity have often faltered, weighed down by the expectation that we must first achieve a perfect doctrinal agreement before we can share at the Lord's table. But I have become increasingly convinced that the path to unity is not paved by human negotiation or theological perfection — it is given to us as a gift at the Eucharistic table of Christ.

In writing this book, I do not make light of the valuable work done in ecumenical dialogues; I deeply respect and honor those ongoing efforts. Yet I believe those dialogues will move more easily and bear greater fruit **once we are one in communion** — because it is through sharing the one Bread and the one Cup that Christ Himself draws us into deeper unity and leads us, by His Spirit, into the fullness of truth.

I offer this work as **my personal reflection**, not as the official position of the Coptic Orthodox Church. It is written with deep love and respect for my Church and all Christian traditions. I pray that its insights may one day be reviewed, discerned, and perhaps even embraced by the Holy Synod of the Coptic Orthodox Church as well as by the governing authorities of other churches, as together we seek the unity for which Christ prayed.

I hope that this book will invite Christians of all backgrounds to look again at the heart of our faith, to rediscover the meaning of the Eucharist, and to embrace the possibility that unity is nearer than we often think — because

Christ Himself is present and active among us. I pray that these pages stir in each reader a renewed love for the Eucharist and a deeper commitment to the unity that Christ desires.

To God alone be the glory.

Hegumen Abraam Sleman
New Jersey, USA, May 3, 2025

Introduction

There is hope for the unity of Christ's Church — a hope anchored not in human strategies or perfect agreement but in the living presence of Christ, who gathers His people at His table. It is at the Eucharist, where we partake of the one Bread and the one Cup, that we are made one Body in Him and are led, by the Holy Spirit, toward the fullness of faith.

This book, *The Eucharist: The Heart of Christian Unity*, invites Christians to rediscover the profound truth that we do not need to wait for perfect doctrinal agreement before we come together in communion. Rather, it is **in communion itself** that we are drawn into true unity and led toward the unity of faith. The Eucharist is not just a sign of unity already accomplished — it is the very means by which Christ unites His people, overcomes division, and builds His Church in love and truth.

Across the chapters, this book explores the biblical foundations of the Eucharist, its meaning in the life of the early Church, the theological insights of the Church Fathers, and the historical wounds that have divided the Body of Christ. It reflects on why efforts to achieve unity by doctrine alone have often failed and shows how a renewed understanding of Eucharistic communion offers a hopeful path forward. Along the way, the book invites readers to envision a Church where the unity that Christ desires is not postponed but lived, nourished and strengthened at His table.

Because the theme of Eucharistic unity touches so many theological, pastoral, and historical dimensions, certain core insights will appear more than once throughout the chapters. These repetitions are intentional — meant to deepen reflection, reinforce key truths, and approach the central message from different perspectives. I hope that, like a repeated refrain in a sacred hymn, these echoes will impress the heart of the message more deeply and draw the reader into greater spiritual reflection.

May these reflections inspire all Christians — across traditions, languages, and cultures — to embrace the Eucharist as the true heart of our unity, trusting that through communion, Christ Himself will lead us into the fullness of faith and love He prayed for.

Chapter 1

Eucharist's Foreshadows in the Old Testament

The Eucharist, as instituted by the Lord Jesus Christ, is not an isolated event in the New Testament but is deeply rooted in the Old Testament. Throughout salvation history, God prefigured the sacrament of the Eucharist in various ways, preparing His people to receive the true Bread of Life. These prefigurations point to Christ as the fulfillment of the divine plan and reveal the richness of the Eucharist as the sacrament of unity.

In this chapter, we will explore four significant Old Testament foreshadowing of the Eucharist: The bread and wine of Melchizedek, the Passover Lamb, the manna from heaven, and the prophetic vision of the eschatological banquet. Each of these serves as a signpost leading to the ultimate fulfillment in Christ and His sacramental presence in the Eucharist.

1. The Bread and Wine of Melchizedek

In the journey of Abram's faith and obedience, Genesis 14 presents a remarkable encounter with a mysterious figure — Melchizedek, the king of Salem and priest of God Most High. After Abram's victorious return from battle, this priestly king brings out bread and wine and blesses Abram in the name of the Most High God. Though his appearance in Scripture is brief, Melchizedek's actions carry immense theological weight. His priesthood, his offering, and his blessing prefigure a greater reality to be fully revealed in Christ, the true King of righteousness and peace.

> And Melchizedek, king of Salem, brought out bread and wine; now he was a priest of God Most High. Then he blessed him and said,
> "Blessed be Abram of God Most High,
> Possessor of heaven and earth" (Genesis 14:18-19).

One of the earliest and most profound foreshadowing of the Eucharist is found in this priestly act of Melchizedek. As both **king and priest**, Melchizedek appears suddenly in Scripture without recorded lineage—pointing to a divine archetype fulfilled in Jesus Christ (Hebrews 7:1-3). He offers bread and wine, not as a common gesture of hospitality but as a sacred act that anticipates the sacrament of Christ's own Body and Blood.

Melchizedek as a Type of Christ

The figure of Melchizedek has long captivated the hearts and minds of biblical scholars, theologians, and the early Church Fathers. Though he appears only briefly in the Genesis narrative, his role is profound. He is introduced without genealogy, without recorded beginning or end, as "king of Salem" and "priest of God Most High" (Genesis 14:18). This mysterious figure is more than a historical character; he is a theological signpost pointing forward to a greater and eternal reality—the person of Jesus Christ.

The Epistle to the Hebrews draws this connection with extraordinary clarity and authority. Referring to Psalm 110:4, the author writes,

> "You are a priest forever,
> According to the order of Melchizedek" (Hebrews 7:17).

This Psalm, originally attributed to King David, prophetically speaks of a priestly figure whose office is not inherited by bloodline, as with the Levitical priesthood, but is established by divine oath and eternal decree. The priesthood of Melchizedek is not limited by time, genealogy, or temple — it is a heavenly priesthood ordained directly by God.

In the Lord Jesus Christ, this priesthood finds its perfect fulfillment. As the eternal Son of God, born not from the tribe of Levi but from the line of Judah, Christ could not serve under the Levitical priesthood. Yet, as Hebrews explains, He was appointed by God as a priest "after the order of Melchizedek," not on the basis of a legal requirement concerning physical descent, "but according to the power of an indestructible life" (Hebrews 7:16). Christ's priesthood, like Melchizedek's, is not bound by the old covenant but transcends it, ushering in a new and everlasting covenant.

Unlike the Levitical priests who offered repeated sacrifices of animals, Christ, the true High Priest, offers Himself once for all. He does not bring bread and wine as mere symbols, as Melchizedek did, but transforms these elements into His very Body and Blood — offered for the life of the world (John 6:51). At the Last Supper, Jesus took bread, gave thanks, broke it, and gave it to His disciples, saying, "Take, eat; this is My body." Then He took the cup, gave thanks, and said, "Drink from it, all of you; for this is My blood of the covenant, which is poured out for many for the forgiveness of sins" (Matthew 26:26–28).

In this act, Jesus not only fulfills the typology of Melchizedek but inaugurates the sacrament of the Eucharist — a perpetual memorial and real participation in His once-for-all sacrifice. As Melchizedek blessed Abram with bread and wine and invoked the blessing of God Most High, so Christ blesses

His people through the Eucharistic offering, drawing them into communion with Himself and with the Father.

Thus, Melchizedek stands as a sacred type, a shadow cast by the radiant light of Christ. He prepares the eyes of faith to recognize in Jesus not only the fulfillment of prophetic expectation but the embodiment of divine priesthood — eternal, powerful, and redemptive. Through this priesthood, believers are brought into the heavenly sanctuary, where Christ intercedes forever on their behalf (Hebrews 7:25) and where His sacrifice continues to bear fruit in the mystery of the Eucharist.

The Significance of Bread and Wine:

Among all the sacrificial elements and offerings in the Old Testament, the act of presenting **bread and wine** is both exceptional and profoundly symbolic. While the Mosaic Law later instituted a detailed system of animal sacrifices, grain offerings, and drink libations, the account of Melchizedek predates the Law and offers something far more enigmatic. Bread and wine — simple, nourishing elements — appear not in the context of atonement or purification but in the setting of blessing and covenantal affirmation. Their introduction through Melchizedek is a prophetic gesture, a shadow of something greater to come.

This offering stands alone in the Old Testament. Melchizedek, priest of God Most High, presents not a slain animal but the very staples of human sustenance — **bread and wine** — and he does so in a priestly act that blesses Abram, the father of the faithful. The Church has long understood this moment not as an isolated event but as a divine foreshadowing of the **Eucharist**, in which Christ, the true High Priest, offers

Himself under the forms of bread and wine for the life and salvation of the world.

The early Church Fathers were quick to recognize the typological depth of Melchizedek's offering. For them, this moment in Genesis was not merely historical but sacramental, pointing forward to the mysteries unveiled in Christ.

St. Cyprian of Carthage, in his celebrated *Epistle 63*, reflects: "In the priest Melchizedek, we see a prefiguration of the sacrament of the Eucharist. He who was a priest of God offered not a lamb, not a goat, but bread and wine, just as Christ, our High Priest, would offer in fulfillment of the New Covenant."

This profound interpretation reveals how the Holy Spirit, even in the earliest pages of Scripture, was already unveiling the shape of redemptive worship that would culminate in Christ. The bread and wine offered by Melchizedek do not stand in contrast to animal sacrifices but transcend them, pointing to a higher reality in which the substance of the offering is not something external to God but God Himself.

At the Last Supper, Jesus gave new and eternal meaning to these ancient elements. He took bread, gave thanks, broke it, and said, "This is My body which is given for you. Do this in remembrance of Me." And in the same way, He took the cup after they had eaten, saying, "This cup which is poured out for you is the new covenant in My blood" (Luke 22:19-20). Thus, Christ takes the very elements first used by Melchizedek and infuses them with divine substance, making them the visible signs of His invisible grace.

Bread and wine become more than symbols—they are the **means** through which Christ imparts His life. In them, the

Church receives Christ's Body and Blood, the eternal priestly offering that unites heaven and earth. This offering is no longer the shadow seen in Melchizedek but the substance found in Christ. The Eucharist thus becomes the fulfillment of the priestly mystery prefigured in Salem—the city of peace—where Melchizedek once reigned.

Moreover, the spiritual richness of these elements cannot be overstated. **Bread** speaks of sustenance, daily provision, and the incarnate Word who said, "I am the bread of life" (John 6:35). **Wine** signifies joy, covenant, and the poured-out blood of Christ, "the fruit of the vine" which He will drink anew with His people in the kingdom of God (Matthew 26:29). Together, they proclaim the fullness of salvation: nourishment and celebration, sacrifice and communion, death and resurrection.

Melchizedek's offering is, therefore, a sacred sign—a veiled announcement of the mystery to come. And in the Church's Eucharistic celebration, that mystery is unveiled. The bread and wine become the table of Christ's sacrifice and the banquet of divine fellowship. What Melchizedek did in shadow, Christ has fulfilled in truth.

2. The Passover Lamb

The institution of the Passover in Exodus 12 is one of the clearest Old Testament foreshadowing of the Eucharist:

> "Now this day will be a memorial to you, and you shall celebrate it as a feast to Yahweh; throughout your generations, you are to celebrate it as a permanent statute" (Exodus 12:14).

On the night of Israel's deliverance from Egypt, each household was commanded to sacrifice an unblemished lamb, spread its blood on the doorposts, and eat its flesh with unleavened bread.

Christ as the True Passover Lamb:

The New Testament explicitly identifies the Lord Jesus as the fulfillment of the Passover: "For Christ, our Passover Lamb, has been sacrificed" (1 Corinthians 5:7). Just as the blood of the lamb saved Israel from physical death, so Christ's Blood saves us from eternal death (John 1:29).

At the Last Supper, the Lord Jesus transformed the meaning of the Passover meal by offering Himself as the true sacrificial Lamb, saying: "This is My body… This is My blood, the blood of the covenant" (Matthew 26:26-28).

Eating the Lamb and the Eucharist:

The Israelites had to eat the flesh of the Passover lamb; merely sacrificing it was not enough. This foreshadows Christ's command: "Unless you eat the flesh of the Son of Man and drink His blood, you have no life in yourselves" (John 6:53).

St. John Chrysostom wrote: "The Jews were commanded to eat the Passover lamb; this was a type. You, then, have been given the reality. The Lamb was sacrificed for you, and you are given His flesh to eat, that the type may be fulfilled in the truth" (Homily on Matthew 82:4).

In the Eucharist, we participate in the true Passover—not merely remembering Christ's sacrifice but partaking in the real presence of the Lamb of God.

3. The Manna from Heaven

After their miraculous deliverance from the bondage of Egypt, the Israelites found themselves in the barren wilderness, far from any natural means of survival. It was there, in the stark emptiness of the desert, that Yahweh revealed Himself once again as their faithful Provider. In response to their hunger and grumbling, Yahweh spoke to Moses, declaring, **"Behold, I will rain bread from heaven for you"** (Exodus 16:4). True to His word, each morning, the Israelites awoke to find a fine, flaky substance covering the ground, which they called "manna," meaning "What is it?" — a testament to its mysterious and heavenly origin.

This daily provision of manna was far more than mere sustenance; it was a divine sign, a foreshadowing of a greater and eternal nourishment yet to be revealed. The manna from heaven pointed forward to the true Bread of Life, the Lord Jesus Christ, who would come down from heaven not merely to sustain physical bodies but to grant eternal life to all who believe in Him.

The Lord Jesus Identifies Himself as the True Manna:

Centuries later, as the Jews reflected upon the greatness of their forefathers' experience in the wilderness, they revered the manna as the ultimate symbol of God's provision. Yet, when confronted with the miraculous feeding of the five thousand, they challenged Jesus, seeking another sign: **"Our fathers ate the manna in the wilderness; as it is written, 'He gave them bread out of heaven to eat'"** (John 6:31).

In response, Jesus unveiled the profound mystery that the manna had only prefigured. He corrected their understanding, saying, "Truly, truly, I say to you, it is not Moses who has given you the bread out of heaven, but My Father gives you the true bread out of heaven. For the bread of God is that which comes down out of heaven and gives life to the world" (John 6:32–33).

Then, in one of the most powerful self-revelations recorded in Scripture, Jesus declared, **"I am the bread of life; he who comes to Me will not hunger, and he who believes in Me will never thirst"** (John 6:35). Whereas the manna sustained the Israelites for a day, Christ, the true Bread from heaven, gives eternal sustenance, satisfying the deepest hunger of the human soul with Himself. As He further revealed, **"I am the living bread that came down out of heaven; if anyone eats of this bread, he will live forever; and the bread also which I will give for the life of the world is My flesh"** (John 6:51).

Participation in the True Bread:

The Lord's teaching culminates in the call to partake of His very Body and Blood, the new and greater manna, given in the sacrament of the Eucharist. **"This is the bread which came down out of heaven—not as the fathers ate and died; the one who eats this bread will live forever"** (John 6:58). Unlike the manna, which, though heavenly, perished with the passing of the day, the true Bread gives everlasting life to those who receive it with faith.

The early Church Fathers deeply perceived this connection between the manna and the Eucharist. St. Ambrose of Milan, in his treatise *On the Mysteries*, wrote, **"The manna was a shadow of the future Eucharist. The bread that you receive is the very Body of Christ. It is not mere bread, but that which Christ has made sacred by His blessing"** (*On the Mysteries* 9:53). For Ambrose, the miraculous provision of the Old

Covenant was but dim anticipation of the wondrous mystery Christ instituted at the Last Supper.

Thus, in the Eucharist, Christ offers not just physical nourishment but His own divine life. Those who eat the true Bread participate in the very life of the risen Christ, being united to Him in a communion that transcends the temporal and ushers them into the eternal. The wilderness journey of the Israelites, sustained by the manna, finds its true and ultimate fulfillment in the pilgrimage of the Church, nourished by the Body and Blood of the Savior on the way to the Promised Land of everlasting life.

4. The Prophetic Hope: "A Table Prepared Before Me"

Throughout the Scriptures, especially in the Psalms and Prophets, we find a recurring image of divine hospitality: the image of a table prepared by God Himself, where He gathers His people to nourish them with His presence. This image is not merely poetic; it is profoundly prophetic, foreshadowing the mystery of the Eucharist—a sacred banquet of communion with God, fulfilled in Christ and anticipated in glory.

In Psalm 23, a psalm beloved for its intimate portrayal of Yahweh as the Shepherd, David exclaims, **"You prepare a table before me in the presence of my enemies; You have anointed my head with oil; my cup overflows"** (Psalm 23:5). This table is not one set in ease or luxury but in the very midst of adversity. It is a declaration that even when surrounded by darkness, God invites His faithful to sit at His table, partake of His goodness, and experience the peace of His presence. For the Church, this table finds its ultimate expression in the

Eucharist, where Christ prepares for us a feast of victory over sin, death, and the enemy of our souls.

Isaiah's Vision of the Messianic Banquet:

The prophet Isaiah lifts the veil of time and sees a glorious day when Yahweh will gather all nations to a divine banquet — one that not only satisfies physical hunger but triumphs over death itself. **"Now Yahweh of hosts will prepare on this mountain a lavish banquet for all peoples, a banquet of aged wine, choice pieces with marrow, and refined aged wine. And on this mountain, He will swallow up the covering which is over all peoples… He will swallow up death for all time"** (Isaiah 25:6–8).

This prophetic vision is fulfilled in Jesus Christ. Through His death and resurrection, the veil of death has been torn, and the way into eternal communion has been opened. In every celebration of the Eucharist, the Church enters into Isaiah's mountain-top feast — not as a future hope only, but as a present participation in the victory of Christ. As we approach the altar, we do so at the invitation of the Lord, who has conquered death and set before us a table of life.

The Eucharist as the Foretaste of the Heavenly Banquet:

The Eucharist is not merely a commemoration of the past but a present and living reality that draws the Church into the eternal. It is a foretaste of the Kingdom that is to come, a moment in which time and eternity meet, and the faithful are given a share in the heavenly joy promised to the saints. The Apostle John, in his vision of the end of all things, hears the proclamation: **"Blessed are those who are invited to the marriage supper of the Lamb"** (Revelation 19:9).

This is the final and glorious banquet — where Christ, the Lamb who was slain, is united forever with His Bride, the Church. But this supper is not merely a future celebration. In every Eucharist, the Church participates in this eschatological mystery. The table of the Lord is the place where heaven and earth are joined, where the Church militant on earth and the Church triumphant in heaven commune around the one Body and the one Cup.

St. Augustine, with his usual spiritual depth, urges believers to recognize the heavenly reality revealed in the Eucharist: "Recognize in this bread what hung on the Cross, and in this cup what flowed from His side. Whatever is announced in this meal is also proclaimed in the heavens" (*Sermon 272*). For Augustine, the Eucharist was not just a sacred ritual — it was the proclamation of the whole Gospel, the memorial of Christ crucified, and the unveiling of the heavenly liturgy.

Living in the Hope of the Table:

Each time we come to the table of the Lord, we are not merely remembering a past sacrifice but participating in a present mystery and living in a future hope. The Eucharist sustains the Church on her pilgrimage, just as manna sustained Israel in the wilderness. But it does more — it lifts the eyes of the faithful to the final restoration, to the day when Christ will return, and God will be "all in all" (1 Corinthians 15:28).

In the Eucharist, the prophetic hope of Scripture is not postponed; it is tasted. The table prepared in the wilderness, the banquet on the mountain, and the marriage supper of the Lamb—all these are made present in the breaking of the bread. The Church lives between the already and the not yet, but at the altar of Christ, the veil between time and eternity grows thin.

Conclusion

The Eucharist is deeply rooted in the Old Testament, fulfilling God's plan revealed in types and shadows. From Melchizedek's offering to the Passover lamb to the Manna from heaven and the Prophetic vision of the Messianic banquet, we see the Eucharist as the ultimate means by which God unites His people.

As the Church, we are called to approach the Eucharist not as a mere doctrine but as the living mystery of Christ's real presence—given to us so that we may be one in Him.

Chapter 2

Institution of the Eucharist

The Eucharist is not a mere human tradition or symbolic ritual; the Father institutes it through Christ Himself as the means by which His followers participate in Christ's life, death, and resurrection. This chapter explores four key moments in Scripture that reveal God's intention for the Eucharist:

1- The Last Supper, where the Lord Jesus establishes the sacrament.

2- The New Covenant in His Blood, fulfilling the prophecy of Jeremiah.

3- The Breaking of Bread in Emmaus, revealing His real presence.

4- The Bread of Life Discourse, where the Lord Jesus proclaims the necessity of eating His flesh and drinking His blood.

Through these biblical accounts, we see that the Eucharist is not just a memorial but a true participation in Christ, who continues to give Himself to the Church.

1. The Lord Jesus' Words at the Last Supper

The foundation of the Church's Eucharistic faith is rooted in the very words of the Lord Jesus at the Last Supper. On the night He was betrayed, Christ gathered with His disciples not only to share a final meal but to inaugurate the New Covenant through the giving of His own Body and Blood. In this sacred moment, He instituted the Eucharist as a perpetual sacrament — the mystery through which He would remain truly present with His Church and unite His followers in one communion.

The accounts in the Synoptic Gospels provide a unified and solemn testimony of this institution, while the writings of the early Church Fathers confirm that the first generations of Christians understood these words not symbolically but literally — as the real and living presence of Christ in the Eucharist.

Narrative of the Synoptic Gospels:

The celebration of the Eucharist finds its origin in the very words and actions of the Lord Jesus at the Last Supper. On the eve of His Passion, Christ instituted the Eucharist not as a mere symbolic memorial but as the real and enduring gift of Himself — His Body and Blood — for the life of the world. This sacred moment, recorded in all three Synoptic Gospels, reveals the foundation of Christian unity and communion with God.

Matthew 26:26–29: "Now while they were eating, Lord Jesus took some bread, and after a blessing, He broke it and gave it to the disciples, and said, 'Take, eat; this is My body.' And when He had taken a cup and given thanks, He gave it to them, saying, 'Drink from it, all of you; for this is My blood of the covenant, which is being poured out for many for the forgiveness of sins. But I say to you, I will not drink of this fruit of the vine from now on until that day when I drink it with you new in My Father's kingdom.'"

The words of the Lord Jesus are clear and unambiguous:

"This is My body" — not a metaphor or a symbol, but His actual Body given for us.

"This is My blood of the covenant" — intentionally echoing the Old Testament sacrifice and covenant ratification (cf. Exodus 24:8), now fulfilled in His redemptive act.

Mark 14:22-25 and Luke 22:19-20 echo this sacred institution nearly word for word, affirming a consistent apostolic tradition across the Gospels. The Eucharist, therefore, is not a later invention but the enduring sacrament that Christ Himself instituted.

The Early Church Fathers on the Real Presence:

The earliest witnesses of the Church — those who lived within a generation or two of the apostles — affirmed the real presence of Christ in the Eucharist. They received the Lord's words with reverence and literal faith.

St. Ignatius of Antioch (d. 107 AD) wrote:

> "They abstain from the Eucharist and prayer because they do not confess that the Eucharist is the flesh of our Savior Lord Jesus Christ, which suffered for our sins and which the Father, in His goodness, raised up again" (Letter to the Smyrnaeans 7).

St. Justin Martyr (2nd century) testified:

> "We call this food Eucharist, and no one else is permitted to partake of it, except one who believes... For we do not receive these things as common bread and common drink; but just as Lord Jesus Christ our Savior, having been made flesh by the Word of God,

took both flesh and blood for our salvation, so we have been taught that the food consecrated by the word of prayer is the flesh and blood of that same incarnate Lord Jesus"(First Apology 66).

From the very beginning, the Church believed and proclaimed that the Eucharist is not merely bread and wine — it is the true Body and Blood of Christ. In this sacred mystery, the faithful partake of divine life and are united with one another as members of His Body, the Church.

2. The Eucharist as the New Covenant in His Blood

The Eucharist is not only a sacrament of communion, but also the fulfillment of the New Covenant prophesied in the Old Testament.

The Prophecy of Jeremiah:

Jeremiah 31:31-34 speaks of a new covenant, one that is not written on tablets of stone but engraved on the hearts of believers:

> "Behold, days are coming, declares Yahweh, when I will make a new covenant with the house of Israel and the house of Judah… I will put My law within them and write it on their heart, and I will be their God, and they shall be My people."

The Lord Jesus explicitly connects the Eucharist to this New Covenant:

> "For I received from the Lord that which I also delivered to you, that the Lord Jesus, on the night when He was betrayed, took bread; and when He had given thanks, He broke it and said, 'This is My body, which is for you; do this in remembrance of Me.' In the same way, He also took the cup after supper, saying, 'This cup is the new covenant in My blood; do this, as often as you drink it, in remembrance of Me'" (1 Corinthians 11:23-26).

St. Paul affirms that the Eucharist is not a human tradition but a direct **command from the Lord Himself**. The phrase **"New Covenant in My Blood"** reveals that the Eucharist is the means by which believers enter into this covenant with God.

The Blood of Christ and the Covenant:

The Eucharist is intimately tied to the covenant relationship between God and His people. In the Old Covenant, as recorded in the book of Exodus, Moses sealed the covenant between Yahweh and Israel by the ritual sprinkling of sacrificial blood upon the altar and the people. Scripture recounts:

> "So Moses took the blood and sprinkled it on the people, and said, 'Behold the blood of the covenant, which Yahweh has made with you in accordance with all these words'" (Exodus 24:8).

This act signified the binding relationship between God and His chosen people, a relationship sealed through the shedding of blood — a vivid reminder that life itself was consecrated to God.

In the New Covenant, the Lord Jesus fulfills and transcends this ancient rite. At the Last Supper, He does not sprinkle the blood of animals but offers His own Blood, poured out for the forgiveness of sins and the reconciliation of humanity to God. He declares to His disciples:

> "Drink from it, all of you; for this is My blood of the covenant, which is being poured out for many for the forgiveness of sins" (Matthew 26:27–28).

Through the offering of His own Body and Blood, Christ establishes an everlasting covenant — one that unites all who believe in Him into a living communion with God. The Eucharist, then, is far more than a memorial; it is the ongoing sign and reality of this eternal covenant. Every time the Church gathers around the altar, it participates anew in the covenantal relationship Christ has inaugurated, fulfilling what was foreshadowed in the Old Testament and fully revealed in the mystery of His sacrificial love.

3. The Breaking of Bread in Emmaus and Christ's Real Presence

The journey to Emmaus is one of the most profound resurrection accounts in the Gospels, rich with mystery, longing, and revelation. As recorded in **Luke 24:13-35**, two disciples were walking from Jerusalem to the village of Emmaus on the very day that the women discovered the empty tomb. Grieved and confused, they spoke about all that had happened—Jesus' crucifixion, the news of His resurrection—when suddenly, **"Jesus Himself approached and began traveling with them. But their eyes were kept from recognizing Him"** (Luke 24:15-16).

The Lord walked with them, opened the Scriptures to them, and explained how all things written about the Christ in the Law, the Prophets, and the Psalms pointed to His suffering and glory. Yet still, their eyes remained closed. It was not until He entered their home and reclined at the table with them that the great unveiling occurred.

> "And it happened that when He had reclined at the table with them, He took the bread and blessed it, and after breaking it, He was giving it to them. Then their eyes were opened, and they recognized Him. And He vanished from their sight." (Luke 24:30-31).

The Eucharist Reveals Christ:

It is no coincidence that the moment of recognition came at the breaking of the bread. Though the disciples had heard His words and felt their hearts burn within them as He opened the Scriptures, it was **in the act of breaking bread**—a deeply Eucharistic gesture—that their eyes were opened. The same Christ who had broken bread at the Last Supper now revealed Himself through the same sacred act.

Here, we are given a glimpse into the mystery of the Eucharist: **Christ is made truly present in the breaking of the bread**. As at Emmaus, He may no longer be seen in bodily form, but He is no less present. His departure from their sight at the very moment of recognition was not a disappearance but a transformation of presence. He remained with them—not physically, but sacramentally.

What occurred at Emmaus is what happens in every celebration of the Eucharist: Christ walks with His people, opens the Scriptures to their understanding, and reveals

Himself in the breaking of the bread. His Real Presence is no less real than it was that evening in Emmaus. Though our eyes may not behold Him in visible form, **faith discerns Him in the sacramental mystery.**

Patristic Insight:

The early Church Fathers understood this Emmaus encounter as a foundational witness to the Real Presence of Christ in the Eucharist. **St. Augustine**, reflecting on this very passage, wrote with profound clarity:

> "He was known in the breaking of the bread. If we desire to know Christ, let us partake of His Body, for He dwells with us in this mystery." (Sermon 234).

St. Augustine emphasized that true knowledge of Christ is not merely intellectual or historical but **sacramental**. To "know" Christ is to encounter Him — truly and spiritually — in the mystery of His Body and Blood. The breaking of the bread, then, is not symbolic alone; it is revelatory. It unveils Christ to the faithful and draws them into communion with Him.

A Living Encounter:

The Emmaus story is more than an ancient account; it is a pattern of the Church's Eucharistic life. Week after week, the Church gathers like the two disciples — often weary, often troubled — bringing their questions and longings to the table of the Lord. There, Christ joins them. He speaks in the Scriptures, He is recognized in the breaking of the bread, and He abides with them through His sacramental presence.

Though He vanishes from the eyes of the flesh, **He remains present in the eyes of faith**, nourishing His people with His very life. In the Eucharist, Emmaus is not a place in history but a living experience. Christ still walks with His Church, still opens the Scriptures, and still reveals Himself in the breaking of the bread.

4. Jesus' Teaching on the Bread of Life

Among the Lord Jesus' many teachings, none is more direct and more theologically profound concerning the sacrament of the Eucharist than His discourse in **John 6**. As He delivered after the miraculous feeding of the five thousand, this teaching elevates the physical miracle to a spiritual reality, pointing His listeners to a heavenly food—one that gives not temporary sustenance but **eternal life**. At the heart of His message is a bold and stunning claim: that **He Himself is the true Bread from heaven** and that **His flesh and blood are the source of life for the world:**

> "I am the bread of life. Your fathers ate the manna in the wilderness, and they died. This is the bread which comes down from heaven, so that one may eat of it and not die. I am the living bread that came down from heaven; if anyone eats of this bread, he will live forever; and also the bread which I will give for the life of the world is My flesh" (John 6:48–51).

This declaration was not a metaphorical statement to be softened or explained away. Instead, Jesus intensified His words, pressing His hearers to grasp the full weight of His message:

> "Truly, truly, I say to you, unless you eat the flesh of the Son of Man and drink His blood, you have no life in yourselves. He who eats My flesh and drinks My

blood has eternal life, and I will raise him up on the last day" (John 6:53-54).

Here, the Lord identifies Himself not only as the provider of life but as the **very substance** of the life He gives. The Eucharist is not a distant sign or symbol but **an actual participation in His flesh and blood** — a communion with the incarnate Christ, the Son of the living God.

The Controversy and the Literal Meaning:

Unsurprisingly, this teaching provoked a deep controversy. Even among those who had followed Jesus and witnessed His miracles, many began to question Him. **"This is a difficult statement,"** they said. **"Who can listen to it?"** (John 6:60). They could not fathom how one could **eat the flesh** and **drink the blood** of a man, even one as revered as the Rabbi from Nazareth.

Yet rather than retract His words or soften the message into a metaphor, Jesus **reinforced the literal truth** of His teaching. He allowed many to walk away — because to deny this mystery would be to deny the very heart of His redemptive mission. As the Gospel records, **"As a result of this, many of His disciples went away and were not walking with Him anymore"** (John 6:66).

Turning to the Twelve, Jesus asked, **"Do you also want to go?"** And it was Peter — always the first among equals — who responded not with full understanding but with **faith**:

> "Lord, to whom shall we go? You have words of eternal life. 69 And we have believed and have come to know that You are the Holy One of God" (John 6:68-69).

Peter's confession remains the model for the Church. The Eucharistic sacrament cannot be understood by natural reason alone; it must be received in faith as the very gift of Christ, grounded in His truth and sealed by His promise.

Patristic Witness:

The early Church, rooted in the apostolic witness, took the Lord's words seriously and literally. For the Fathers, the Eucharist was not a symbol or abstraction but the **real Body and Blood of Christ** consecrated and given for the life of the faithful.

St. Cyril of Jerusalem, writing in the fourth century, boldly exhorted the newly baptized to approach the mystery with faith, not doubt:

> "Do not doubt whether this is true but rather receive the words of the Savior in faith. For He, being the Truth, does not lie when He says: 'This is My Body.'" (*Mystagogical Catecheses 4:1–6*)

For St. Cyril and the Church in every generation that followed in his footsteps, the words of Christ were not open to reinterpretation. He who turned water into wine at Cana can and does transform bread and wine into His very Body and Blood. This transformation—though hidden from the eyes of flesh—is revealed to the eyes of faith and experienced in the depths of the soul.

The Life-Giving Mystery:

To partake of the Eucharist, then, is to enter into a mystery of love, sacrifice, and divine communion. It is to eat and drink Christ—not merely to remember Him, but to receive Him.

Through this sacrament, believers receive **His life**, are united with **His death and resurrection**, and are assured of being raised **with Him on the last day**.

The Bread of Life is Christ Himself. He offers Himself daily at the altar, calling each of us not merely to understand but to come, to believe, and to receive.

Conclusion

The Eucharist stands at the very heart of the Christian life — not as a human invention, nor as a symbolic gesture, but as the divine gift of God Himself, instituted by the Lord Jesus on the night of His betrayal. From the **Upper Room in Jerusalem** to the **road to Emmaus** and from the **mountain of the Bread of Life discourse** to the **ongoing life of the Church**, the mystery of the Eucharist has been faithfully handed down and received in faith.

We have seen in this chapter how the Eucharist was established by Christ at the Last Supper as the **New Covenant in His Blood**, fulfilling the ancient promises of the prophets and revealing a new, eternal communion between God and His people. In this sacrament, the Church enters into that covenant again and again — not as a mere remembrance but as a real participation in the life, death, and resurrection of Christ.

In the breaking of the bread at Emmaus, Christ made Himself known, not through explanation, but through presence. The eyes of the disciples were opened not by reasoning but by the mystery. And so it is today: Christ continues to walk with His Church, to open the Scriptures to her, and to reveal Himself at His table.

In the Bread of Life discourse, He spoke plainly, calling His disciples to **eat His flesh and drink His blood**. Many turned away, scandalized by the realism of His words. Yet those who remained—those who believed—discovered the source of eternal life. **"Lord, to whom shall we go? You have the words of eternal life"** (John 6:68). The Eucharist, therefore, is the response of faith to the words and promise of Christ, the Lamb of God who gives Himself to the world.

The Church, from her earliest days, has understood and proclaimed this truth with unwavering conviction. From the apostolic era to the Church Fathers, from the deserts of Egypt to the catacombs of Rome, believers have gathered around the altar, recognizing in the Eucharist the true Body and Blood of the Lord. As **St. Ignatius, St. Justin Martyr, St. Cyril of Jerusalem**, and **St. Augustine** have testified, the Eucharist is not a mere symbol but **the living presence of Christ**—offered, received, and adored.

To approach the Eucharist, then, is to come into communion with God through Christ Himself. It is to be nourished by His divine life, united with His Body, and formed into His likeness. In this sacred mystery, heaven and earth meet, the promises of the prophets are fulfilled, and the Church is sustained on her journey toward the Kingdom.

The Eucharist is the Father's gift through the Son in the power of the Spirit—an eternal covenant sealed with divine blood and celebrated until Christ comes again. In every Mass, every Divine Liturgy, and every gathering around the Lord's table, the Church declares and experiences the mystery: **Christ has died. Christ is risen. Christ will come again.**

Chapter 3

Eucharist and the One Body of Christ

The Eucharist is not only the sacrament of Christ's presence but also the mystery through which the Church is united as the one Body of Christ. The partaking of the **one bread** binds believers into **one body** (1 Corinthians 10:16-17), fulfilling Christ's prayer for unity (John 17:21).

In this chapter, we will explore four key aspects of how the Eucharist relates to the One Body of Christ:

1- The Church as One Body in Christ (Romans 12:5)

2- The Eucharist as Participation in Christ (1 Corinthians 10:16-17)

3- Unity and Love as Conditions for Eucharistic Participation (1 Corinthians 11:17-34)

4- The Role of the Holy Spirit in Eucharistic Consecration and Communion

Through these, we will see that the Eucharist is not a private devotion but a **corporate reality**, drawing all believers into deeper unity with Christ and with one another.

1. The Church as One Body in Christ

From the very beginning of his epistles, the Apostle Paul speaks of the Church not as a scattered assembly of individuals but as a single, living organism—the Body of Christ. This is not a metaphor to be lightly understood; it is a sacred reality. The

Church is one body, and each believer is a member of it, bound together not by shared interest or mere community but by the Spirit of Christ and through the sacrament of His Body and Blood.

St. Paul elaborates, saying:

> "For just as we have many members in one body and all the members do not have the same function, so we, who are many, are one body in Christ, and individually members one of another" (Romans 12:4-5).

Here, the apostle emphasizes not only the unity of the Church but the interdependence of its members. Just as each part of the human body contributes to the life of the whole, so every Christian—baptized into Christ—contributes to the health and function of the Church. This truth is made visible and tangible in the Eucharist.

The Eucharist as the Supreme Expression of Unity:

The Eucharist is not a private act of devotion detached from the life of the Church. Rather, it is the supreme expression of the Church's unity in Christ. In receiving the one Bread and one Cup, believers are not only joined to Christ but also joined to one another. As the Apostle affirms elsewhere:

> "Since there is one bread, we who are many are one body, for we all partake of the one bread" (1 Corinthians 10:17)

This act of communion—both vertical with Christ and horizontal with fellow believers—transforms the gathered community into a single body, the mystical Body of Christ. The

Bread is not only Christ's Body given for us but also the Bread that unites us into His Body, the Church.

St. Paul expands on this in his epistle to the Ephesians, teaching that Christ is the **Head over all things to the Church, which is His Body, the fullness of Him who fills all in all** (Ephesians 1:22-23). This means that when the Church gathers to celebrate the Eucharist, it is not merely remembering Christ's sacrifice—it is being gathered into Christ Himself, who is both the One offered and the One offering, both the Head and the Body.

A Unity That Is Real, Not Merely Symbolic:

In a world where unity is often reduced to sentiment or shared ideals, the Church's unity in the Eucharist stands apart. It is not simply symbolic—it is ontological. Just as the bread and wine become truly and substantially the Body and Blood of Christ, so the Church becomes truly and spiritually one Body in Him.

To receive the Eucharist, then, is not only to enter into communion with Christ but to be bound in real communion with every other member of His Body. This is why division among Christians, especially at the Eucharistic table, wounds the very heart of the Church's identity. The Eucharist proclaims that we are one in Christ; to partake unworthily or in isolation from the Church is to deny that proclamation.

Patristic Insight: St. John Chrysostom

The great preacher of Constantinople, **St. John Chrysostom**, captured the profound connection between the

Eucharist and the unity of the Church with unparalleled clarity:

> "You partake of the Body of Christ to become what you receive. For if He is the Head and we are the Body, then it is the same Body—the one that is offered on the Altar and the one that is the Church." (Homily on 1 Corinthians 24:4)

This remarkable statement highlights the transformative nature of the Eucharist. In receiving Christ, the faithful are not only nourished—they are **conformed** to Christ and **incorporated** more deeply into His Body. The altar and the Church are not two separate realities; they are joined in the same mystery.

The Eucharist as a Proclamation and Participation:

Every Eucharistic celebration is, therefore, a dual act: it is a **proclamation of unity**—that in Christ we are one—and it is a **participation in that unity**, made real through the reception of the Body and Blood of the Lord. In the Eucharist, believers do not merely remember a past event but are drawn into a present communion and an eternal reality. It is the sacrament that builds the Church and keeps her one, holy, catholic, and apostolic.

As such, the Eucharist calls each member of the Body to live in charity, humility, and mutual service. If we partake of one Body, we must also be one in heart. The Eucharist forms the Church, and the Church lives through the Eucharist.

2. The Eucharist as Participation in Christ

> "The cup of blessing that we bless, is it not a sharing in the blood of Christ? The bread that we break, is it not a sharing in the body of Christ?" (1 Corinthians 10:16-17)

With these words, the Apostle Paul unveils a foundational truth of Christian life: the Eucharist is not merely a symbol or remembrance but a **mystical participation** in Christ Himself. The word he uses—**koinonia** (κοινωνία)—expresses something far deeper than a passive memorial. It signifies an intimate, life-giving communion, a real and active sharing in the very Body and Blood of the Lord. This communion is not metaphorical; it is sacramental, profound, and transformative.

The Eucharist, then, is the means by which believers enter into the mystery of Christ's saving Passion and life-giving Resurrection. Through it, we are not only reminded of the sacrifice of Calvary—we are united with it. The same sacrifice once offered on the Cross is made present to us in sacramental form, and we are invited to partake of it with reverence and faith.

Eucharistic Communion as Real Participation:

The mystery of the Eucharist lies in its **dual reality**: it is both sacrificial and unitive. In receiving the consecrated Bread and Wine, we are not simply affirming our faith—we are entering into a **real encounter with Christ**. This sacred meal is not an earthly symbol of a heavenly truth; it is the heavenly truth itself made present on earth.

The **bread we break is not just a sign of unity**; it is the **instrument of unity**, drawing each participant into the crucified and risen life of Christ. Through the Eucharist, believers become **partakers of divine grace**, receiving not only spiritual strength but Christ Himself—His very Body, Blood, Soul, and Divinity. As Paul affirms, **"Because there is one bread, we who are many are one body, for we all partake of the one bread"** (1 Corinthians 10:17).

The Eucharist, therefore, **re-presents** (not merely represents) the sacrifice of Christ. It is the same sacrifice, now offered in an unbloody manner, by which the faithful are mystically united to His death and share in the power of His Resurrection. Every Eucharistic liturgy is a moment in which the eternal enters time, and the Church stands at the foot of the Cross while also beholding the glory of the Risen One.

Patristic Insight:

This profound understanding was clearly articulated by the early Church Fathers, who guarded the mystery of the Eucharist with both theological clarity and pastoral devotion. **St. Cyril of Alexandria**, a towering theologian of the early Church, wrote:

> "When we partake of the Holy Eucharist, we do not receive mere bread and wine; we receive Christ Himself. He dwells in us, and we in Him, forming one spiritual body"(Commentary on John 6:56).

Here, St. Cyril echoes the teaching of Christ in the Gospel of John: **"He who eats My flesh and drinks My blood abides in Me, and I in him"** (John 6:56). This is not merely poetic language; it is theological truth. In the Eucharist, Christ comes to dwell in the believer—not symbolically, but **really and spiritually**, entering into the deepest recesses of the human soul.

St. Cyril's insight affirms that this divine indwelling is not individualistic but ecclesial. Those who receive Christ in the Eucharist are drawn not only into union with Him but into **union with one another**. The Church becomes the Body of Christ not by metaphor or agreement but through sacramental participation in the Eucharist. It is this sacred meal that binds believers together across all divisions of time, language, and nation, making them one in Christ.

The Eucharist: Participation in Divine Life

To receive the Eucharist is to be drawn into the **divine life of the Father**. As Christ is one with the Father, so He draws us into that same unity by the Spirit. The Eucharist is thus not only a sharing in Christ's humanity but in His divine Sonship. It is a participation in the very **life of God**, granted to us by grace and received in faith.

Through the Eucharist, the Church experiences what it means to be "in Christ"—not simply imitating Him, but being united with Him, abiding in Him, and being transformed through Him by the Holy Spirit. It is this transformation, this participation in divine life, that forms the essence of Christian holiness and mission.

In every celebration of the Eucharist, heaven touches earth, and the eternal life of God is poured into the hearts of the faithful. This is why the Church proclaims the Eucharist as the **source and summit** of the Christian life. All that we believe, all that we hope for, and all that we are as the Church flows from this mystery—and returns to it in worship and thanksgiving.

3. Unity and Love as Conditions for Eucharistic Participation

The Eucharist is the sacrament of love and unity—the mystery by which the Church becomes one Body in Christ through partaking of the one Bread. Yet this divine gift comes with a sacred responsibility: to approach the altar in a spirit of communion not only with Christ but also with one another. The Apostle Paul, writing to the Corinthian church, did not hesitate to rebuke those who treated the Lord's Supper as a private meal rather than a holy sacrament. For St. Paul, to divide the Church while claiming to partake of the one Body of Christ was not only a contradiction—it was a **profanation**.

St. Paul's Warning Against Divisions at the Lord's Table:

The Corinthian believers were outwardly gathering for the Eucharist, but inwardly, their divisions and disregard for one another were devastating the integrity of the sacred meal. St. Paul's rebuke is sharp:

> "For, in the first place, when you come together as a church, I hear that divisions exist among you, and in part, I believe it. For there must also be factions among you, so that those who are approved may become evident among you. Therefore, when you meet together in the same place, it is not to eat the Lord's Supper, for in your eating each one takes his

own supper first, and one is hungry, and another is drunk" (1 Corinthians 11:18-21).

The Apostle makes it clear that **where there is no unity, there is no true Eucharist**. It is not enough to repeat the ritual of the Supper. The Eucharist demands the heart to be in communion with Christ and the Church. Those who turn the sacred feast into a display of selfishness or disregard for others, St. Paul warns, are not celebrating the Lord's Supper at all.

To receive the Body of Christ while living in contradiction to the unity and love that it proclaims is to **eat and drink judgment**. The Eucharist is not a private devotion but an ecclesial act—a sacrament of unity. If that unity is broken, and no effort is made toward reconciliation, the celebration becomes hollow and even dangerous.

Receiving Worthily: Love and Unity

St. Paul issues a solemn warning:

> "Therefore, whoever eats the bread or drinks the cup of the Lord in an unworthy manner shall be guilty of the body and the blood of the Lord. But a man must test himself, and in so doing, he is to eat of the bread and drink of the cup. For he who eats and drinks, eats and drinks judgment to himself if he does not judge [discern] the body rightly" (1 Corinthians 11:27-29).

To "**discern the body**" means more than simply believing in the Real Presence of Christ in the Eucharist. It also means **recognizing the Church**—the Body of Christ—as an inseparable reality. One cannot claim to commune with Christ while ignoring, wounding, or excluding His members. Every act of reception is, therefore, a call to examine not only our personal holiness but also our relationships within the Body.

Worthily receiving the Eucharist does not imply being perfect, but being repentant—coming to the altar with humility, contrition, and love. It means choosing forgiveness over resentment, reconciliation over division, and unity over self-interest. The one who approaches in this spirit is truly prepared to receive the gift of Christ's Body and Blood.

The Eucharist as a Call to Reconciliation

The Eucharist is not only a celebration of unity—it is also a **call to unity**. Before the gifts are brought forward before the Bread is broken, the believer must ask:

- Am I at peace with my brother?

- Do I love as Christ has loved me?

- Have I forgiven as I have been forgiven?

This self-examination is not optional; it is essential. The Lord Himself taught:

> "Therefore, if you are presenting your offering at the altar, and there remember that your brother has something against you, leave your offering there before the altar and go; first be reconciled to your brother, and then come and present your offering" (Matthew 5:23–24).

To offer worship while holding onto bitterness is to deny the very heart of the Gospel. The Eucharist proclaims the death and resurrection of Christ, the reconciliation of humanity to

God — but it also demands that this reconciliation be lived out in the Church.

Patristic Insight:

This truth was powerfully echoed by **St. Augustine**, who reminded his flock of the personal and communal dimension of Eucharistic communion:

> "If you want to receive life from the Eucharist, first examine yourself: Do you live in peace with your brothers? The Eucharist is the sacrament of unity — do not approach with division in your heart." (Sermon 272)

For St. Augustine, as for St. Paul, the Eucharist is not only a sacrament of the presence of Christ but of the **unity of the Church**. Those who come to the altar without love have not discerned the Body. Those who refuse to forgive are not prepared to receive the Bread of forgiveness. The altar is not a place of concealment but of truth. In the presence of the crucified and risen Lord, all masks fall away.

A Call to Love

Thus, every celebration of the Eucharist is also a summons — a call to love as Christ loved, to forgive as He forgave, and to strive for the unity that He prayed for: **"That they may all be one, even as You, Father, are in Me and I in You"** (John 17:21). It is not enough to participate in the ritual. The heart must be open. The soul must be reconciled. The mind must be renewed in the love of Christ.

The Eucharist is not just a gift; it is a responsibility. It is not only about communion with Christ — it is about **becoming His**

Body, living in unity, peace, and mutual love. To approach the altar rightly is to come ready to live out what we receive—to be the Body of Christ in the world.

4. The Holy Spirit and the Eucharist: Consecration and Communion

The Eucharist is not merely a sacred ritual preserved from the past. It is a **living mystery**, continually made present in the Church by the power of the **Holy Spirit**. Just as the Holy Spirit overshadowed the Virgin Mary and brought about the Incarnation of the Word, so too it is the Spirit who, in every Divine Liturgy, brings about the **real presence of Christ in the Eucharist** and unites the faithful to Him in communion.

The Holy Spirit in the Eucharistic Consecration:

When the Church gathers to celebrate the Eucharist, she is not re-enacting a past event but participating in the eternal sacrifice of Christ, made present anew by the Holy Spirit. The institution of the Eucharist at the Last Supper was the decisive moment when Christ entrusted this mystery to His disciples. Yet, it is the **Holy Spirit who actualizes it** at every celebration across time and space.

This is clearly expressed in the **Epiclesis**, the solemn invocation of the Holy Spirit in the anaphora of the liturgy. At this moment, the priest stretches out his hands over the gifts and implores the Father to send the Holy Spirit upon the bread and wine:

> "Send down Your Holy Spirit upon us and upon these gifts here set forth. And make this bread the

precious Body of Your Christ, and that which is in this cup the precious Blood of Your Christ..."

In this sacred moment, the bread and wine are not merely blessed—they are **transformed**. They become the very Body and Blood of Christ by the invisible yet powerful working of the Holy Spirit. This mystery is not the work of human effort, eloquence, or symbolism; it is entirely the work of divine grace.

St. John of Damascus, one of the most revered voices of the Eastern Church, articulates this truth with clarity:

> "The bread and wine are changed into the Body and Blood of Christ by the invocation of the Holy Spirit, just as the Holy Spirit came upon the Virgin Mary and brought forth the Incarnate Word" (On the Orthodox Faith 4.13).

This profound analogy between the Incarnation and the Eucharist underscores the central role of the Spirit in both. In both mysteries, the Spirit brings Christ into the world: once in the flesh and now in the sacrament. Just as Mary became the dwelling place of the Incarnate Word by the Spirit, so the Church, by the same Spirit, becomes the bearer of Christ in the Eucharist.

The Holy Spirit in Our Communion with Christ:

The Spirit's role in the Eucharist does not end with consecration. It is **also by the Spirit** that the faithful are drawn into communion with Christ and one another. The Eucharist is not only Christ becoming present on the altar; it is Christ **uniting Himself to us**, and us to Him, in the unity of His Body—the Church.

As St. Paul teaches:

> "For also by one Spirit, we were all baptized into one body, whether Jews or Greeks, whether slaves or free, and we were all made to drink of one Spirit" (1 Corinthians 12:13)

Here, the apostle reminds us that it is the **same Spirit who baptizes and nourishes**. The Spirit makes us members of Christ's Body, and in the Eucharist, we drink of the Spirit who has consecrated the gifts and who sanctifies our souls. This is why the Eucharist is not merely a personal encounter but a **communal and corporate reality**. It is by the Holy Spirit that we become **"one body in Christ,"** united not by mere agreement but by divine grace.

Through the Eucharist, the Holy Spirit works an interior transformation. He unites us more deeply to Christ, purifies our hearts, and shapes us into the image of the Son. In every worthy reception of the Eucharist, the Spirit deepens our sanctification, drawing us into greater love, humility, and unity with the entire Body of believers.

The Spirit of Communion and Holiness:

Thus, the Eucharist is offered to the Father, instituted through the Son, and perfected by the Spirit. It is the Spirit who sanctifies the gifts, the celebrants, and the entire assembly. Without the Spirit, there is no Eucharist and no true communion.

In every Divine Liturgy, the Church prays not only for the transformation of the gifts but for the transformation of the people:

> "Make us all who partake of the one Bread and the one Cup to be united to one another in the communion of the one Holy Spirit."

This prayer encapsulates the essence of Eucharistic life. We receive not simply to be nourished but to be made one — to be transformed into the likeness of Christ and filled with the Spirit of holiness.

The **goal of the Eucharist is communion** — with Christ, with the Father, and with one another, through the indwelling presence of the Spirit. It is the Spirit who lifts our hearts to heaven, unites the earthly liturgy with the heavenly worship, and seals our participation in the eternal life of God.

Conclusion

The mystery of the Eucharist is not only the mystery of Christ's real presence but the mystery of the **Church's real unity** — a unity forged not by human will but by divine grace. In receiving the one Bread and drinking of the one Cup, believers are not engaging in an individual ritual but entering into the very life of the Body of Christ. The Eucharist is the sacrament through which the Church **is nourished, formed, and made one**.

We have seen in this chapter that this unity is not theoretical or symbolic — it is **ontological and sacramental**. It begins with our being baptized into one Body (Romans 12:5), and it is deepened each time we gather at the altar to share in the one Bread and the one Cup (1 Corinthians 10:16-17). The Eucharist does not merely remind us of unity; it **creates** it. It is the act through which the Church becomes what she receives: the Body of Christ.

And yet, this unity comes with a sacred charge. St. Paul warns that to approach the Eucharist with division, selfishness, or unrepented sin is to **profane the Body and Blood of the Lord**. It is not enough to celebrate the Eucharist outwardly; we must be inwardly conformed to its truth. We must **discern the Body**, not only in the sacred gifts but in our brothers and sisters. Without love, the Eucharist is not truly celebrated.

The Eucharist is also the work of the **Holy Spirit**, who sanctifies the gifts and unites the Church. Just as the Spirit brought forth Christ in the womb of the Virgin, so He brings Christ to the altar. Just as the Spirit hovered over the waters at creation, so He hovers over the Eucharistic elements to bring forth new life. And just as the Spirit forms the Church into one Body, He makes us holy through our communion with Christ.

Thus, the Eucharist is the **source and summit** of the Church's unity. It is where heaven meets earth, where division gives way to reconciliation, where individuality is transformed into communion, and where the Church most fully becomes herself. It is the mystery of love made visible — the gift of Christ for the life of the world and the life of His Church.

To partake of the Eucharist worthily is to respond to Christ's prayer: **"That they may all be one"** (John 17:21). It is to embrace the vocation of love, forgiveness, and unity. It is to receive not only the Body of Christ but to become it.

As St. Augustine reminds us:

> "If you are the Body and the members of Christ, it is your mystery that lies upon the altar. Be what you see, and receive what you are" (Sermon 272).

The Eucharist is not just something we celebrate; it is something we become. In every Divine Liturgy, the Church is renewed in her identity as the One Body of Christ—united in faith, sanctified by the Spirit, and sent forth to be Christ's presence in the world.

Let us, then, draw near to this holy mystery with reverence, humility, and love, that we may not only receive Christ but be conformed to Him and one another, in one Body, one Spirit, and one hope of our calling.

Chapter 4

Eucharist as a Unifying Reality in the Early Church

From its earliest days, the Church was a **Eucharistic community**—gathered not merely around preaching, doctrine, or moral instruction but around the **table of the Lord**. The Eucharist was not an optional rite or a symbolic gesture; it was the very **center of Christian life**. In it, the early believers encountered the crucified and risen Christ, shared in His Body and Blood, and were bound together into **one Body by one Spirit**. This sacred meal was not simply an expression of unity—it was the **means** by which unity was created and sustained in the Church.

The early Christians did not see the Eucharist as a private devotion but as a **corporate mystery** in which the whole Church was built up as the Body of Christ. The Eucharist was the **heartbeat of the Church's unity**, a visible and tangible sign of their oneness in Christ. It shaped their daily life, informed their relationships, and guided their understanding of what it meant to be a Church.

This chapter explores how the Eucharist served as the **foundation of Christian unity** in the life of the early Church. Through historical testimony, scriptural reflection, and the voices of the Church Fathers, we will examine how Eucharistic communion was deeply intertwined with ecclesial communion.

In the breaking of the bread, the early believers discerned the living Christ and saw themselves as members of one another. The Eucharist was both a sign and a cause of unity — grounded in truth, sustained by love and made effective by the power of the Holy Spirit.

As we revisit the witness of the early Church, we are reminded that **true Christian unity is Eucharistic at its core**. If we long for the restoration of unity among Christians today, we must return to the same source that united the Church from the beginning: the **Body and Blood of Christ** given for the life of the world.

1. The Believers' Steadfastness in Breaking Bread Together

> "They were continually devoting themselves to the apostles' teaching and to the fellowship, to the breaking of bread and to prayer" (Acts 2:42).

The book of Acts offers a precious glimpse into the life of the **first Christian community** — a community that emerged immediately after the outpouring of the Holy Spirit on the day of Pentecost. These earliest believers, drawn from every nation under heaven, were not united by culture, language, or geography but by a shared faith in the crucified and risen Lord. At the very heart of their common life was a fourfold pattern of devotion: **the apostles' teaching, fellowship (koinonia), the breaking of bread**, and **prayer**.

These were not peripheral activities but the **core structure** of early Christian life. The "breaking of bread" mentioned here is not to be confused with ordinary meals; rather, it is a clear and intentional reference to the **Eucharist** — the sacramental remembrance and real participation in the death and resurrection of Christ.

The Centrality of the Eucharist:

The phrase "they were continually devoting themselves" indicates that the Eucharistic celebration was not sporadic or occasional but **constant and central**. The early Christians did not relegate the Eucharist to feast days or special events. It was the very **heartbeat of the Church's worship**, celebrated with frequency, reverence, and joy. In it, they encountered the living Christ, were nourished by His Body and Blood, and were united to one another in divine love.

The Eucharist was not an **individual act of piety** but a **corporate act of communion**. To partake of the one Bread was to be joined not only to Christ but also to **every other believer who shared in the same mystery**. It was the tangible expression of their oneness in Him—a unity that was both mystical and visible.

Luke further describes this early Eucharistic life in Acts 2:46–47:

"And daily devoting themselves with one accord in the temple and breaking bread from house to house, they were taking their meals together with gladness and sincerity of heart, praising God and having favor with all the people. And the Lord was adding to their number daily those who were being saved."

This passage beautifully captures the atmosphere of early Christian worship: **daily Eucharistic gatherings**, shared meals, joyful hearts, and communal praise. Their unity was not abstract—it was **embodied and enacted** through the Eucharist and flowed into every aspect of their lives.

The Eucharist as the Strength of the Church:

The unity of the early Church was not a distant ideal but a **lived reality**, nourished and sustained through the Eucharist. It was **around the table of the Lord** that believers found the strength to endure persecution, the courage to proclaim the Gospel, and the love to care for one another. Through the Eucharist, there was the **source of their spiritual vitality**, binding them in the one Spirit and enabling them to live as one Body.

This unity was so profound that **Acts 4:32** describes them as being "**of one heart and soul**." This level of harmony and mutual love did not come through human effort alone—it was the **fruit of the Eucharist**, the sacrament of divine charity.

The Eucharist as a Sign of Christian Charity:

For the early Christians, the Eucharist did not exist in isolation from daily life. It shaped their behavior, informed their relationships, and called them to live in love. Just as Christ gave Himself in the sacrament, so too were believers expected to give of themselves in practical acts of mercy.

> "And the congregation of those who believed were of one heart and soul, and not one was saying that any of his possessions was his own, but, for them, everything was common" (Acts 4:32).

"For there was not a needy person among them, for all who were owners of land or houses would sell them and bring the proceeds of the sales and lay them at the apostles' feet, and they would be distributed to each as any had need" (Acts 4:34-35).

Their Eucharistic unity flowed outward into **radical generosity and social solidarity**. The breaking of the bread led to the **breaking down of barriers** — between rich and poor, Jew and Gentile, male and female. The Eucharist revealed that all were one in Christ, and therefore, all were responsible for one another.

Patristic Insight:

The inseparability of Eucharistic worship and Christian charity was eloquently preached by **St. John Chrysostom**, who warned that to receive the Eucharist while ignoring the needs of a fellow believer was a grave contradiction:

> "You have tasted the Blood of the Lord, yet you do not recognize your brother. You dishonor this table when you do not judge worthy of sharing your food someone judged worthy of sharing this meal"(Homily on 1 Corinthians 27:4).

Chrysostom echoes the apostolic concern of St. Paul in 1 Corinthians 11 — that the Eucharist, if received without love, becomes a source of judgment rather than life. For the early Church, unity at the altar demanded unity in daily life. The Eucharist was not only a **mystery to be adored** but a **calling to be lived**.

The Eucharist as a Pattern for Today:

The early Christians understood that **Eucharistic unity must lead to concrete expressions of love and service**. This remains a vital lesson for the Church today. To share in the Body and Blood of Christ is to accept the vocation of unity, to seek reconciliation with others, and to live in self-giving love.

As we reflect on the steadfastness of the first believers in breaking bread together, we are reminded that **Eucharistic communion is not an isolated event** but a way of life. It is a sacrament that calls us into a deeper relationship with Christ and with one another—a communion that transforms the heart, shapes the community, and bears witness to the world.

2. The Didache and the Practice of Eucharistic Communion

Among the earliest extra-biblical Christian writings, the *Didache*—meaning *The Teaching of the Twelve Apostles*—stands as a treasured witness to the faith and practice of the early Church. Composed in the late first or early second century, likely in a Jewish-Christian context within Syria or Palestine, the *Didache* serves as both a catechetical manual for new believers and a liturgical guide for the community. Its brief but profound chapters offer us one of the earliest recorded insights into how the first Christians **celebrated the Eucharist** and how they understood its purpose and power.

Unlike later theological treatises, the *Didache* speaks in the simple and practical language of lived faith. And yet, within its liturgical prayers and instructions, we find a vision of the Eucharist that is rich with meaning: a **sacrament of unity**, a celebration of thanksgiving, and a call to reconciliation.

The Eucharist as a Sacrament of Unity:

One of the most beautiful and theologically profound prayers in the *Didache* is found in chapter 9, which includes a Eucharistic thanksgiving over the bread. It reads:

> "As this broken bread was scattered upon the mountains and was gathered together and became one, so let Your Church be gathered together from the ends of the earth into Your kingdom" (Didache 9:4).

This early liturgical formula evokes a powerful image of Eucharistic unity. Just as many individual grains of wheat, once scattered, are gathered, crushed, kneaded, and baked into one loaf, so too are believers—scattered across the world—gathered into one body in Christ through the Eucharist. This metaphor not only reflects the agricultural setting of ancient Palestine but offers a deep theological truth: the Eucharist is the **means by which the Church is made one**.

The prayer recognizes the Eucharist as a **gathering act**—not just of people in a room, but of the universal Church. Through the Eucharist, the local assembly is mystically joined to the Church across time and space, united in one offering, one Body, and one Spirit. The goal of this Eucharistic unity is eschatological: the final gathering of the Church into the Kingdom of God.

The *Didache's* vision echoes the apostolic teachings of Paul, who declared, **"Because there is one bread, we who are many are one body; for we all partake of the one bread"** (1 Corinthians 10:17). Participation in the Eucharist was never intended to be private or individualistic. From the beginning, it was understood as a communal and corporate act—one that made the many into one in Christ.

Requirements for Eucharistic Participation:

While the Eucharist was a means of uniting the Church, the *Didache* also made clear that this unity required a **spiritual foundation** of faith, baptism, and reconciliation. In *Didache* 9:5, we read:

> "But let no one eat or drink of your Eucharist unless they have been baptized into the name of the Lord."

This short instruction reveals an essential truth: **baptism is the entry point into Eucharistic communion**. The early Church did not separate the Eucharist from the sacramental life. Only those who had been initiated into Christ through baptism were permitted to partake of the sacred meal because only they had been incorporated into His Body.

This practice reflects the apostolic understanding that the Eucharist presupposes a covenant relationship with God and a visible bond with His Church. The Eucharist is not for spectators — it is for **participants**, those who have entered into the life, death, and resurrection of Christ through water and the Spirit.

Moreover, the *Didache* assumes a moral and spiritual preparation for the Eucharist. Though not detailed at length, the context suggests a concern for **reconciliation, purity of heart, and peace with one's neighbor**. The Church Fathers would later expand on this principle, emphasizing the need for confession, repentance, and charity before receiving the Eucharist.

A Deeply Communal Practice:

The Didache confirms that Eucharistic participation in the early Church was not a private experience but a communal celebration grounded in unity and order toward love. The liturgical prayers emphasize not only thanksgiving but also solidarity, forgiveness, and hope for the coming Kingdom. The Eucharist was the center of Christian life—not merely as a ritual to be performed but as a reality to be lived.

This early Christian document, though simple in language, conveys a profound theological truth: the Eucharist is both a **gift** and a **responsibility**. It gathers, sanctifies, and unites the faithful—but it also demands integrity of life, faithfulness to Christ, and love for one another.

Enduring Wisdom from the Ancient Church:

The voice of the *Didache* still speaks to us today. In an age where the Eucharist is often reduced to individual spirituality or seen through the lens of denominational boundaries, the *Didache* reminds us that the Eucharist is the **sacrament of ecclesial communion**. It presupposes a shared faith, a reconciled heart, and a visible bond with the Body of Christ.

Just as the early Christians prayed that the broken bread might symbolize their gathered unity, so too must the Church today long for the restoration of that visible unity—**"from the ends of the earth into God's kingdom."**

In the Eucharist, we are not only nourished—we are gathered, formed, and sent as one Body to proclaim the love of Christ to the world.

3. St. Ignatius of Antioch: "Where the Bishop Is, There Is the Church"

In the early second century, as the Church spread throughout the Roman Empire, one voice stood out as a clear and passionate witness to both the **unity of the Church** and the **centrality of the Eucharist: St. Ignatius of Antioch.** A disciple of the Apostle John and the third bishop of Antioch, St. Ignatius was martyred around A.D. 107 under Emperor Trajan. On his way to Rome to face execution, he wrote seven letters to various Christian communities, letters which have become treasured documents of the early Church.

St. Ignatius' writings are among the earliest post-apostolic testimonies we possess, and they are especially significant for how clearly they articulate the relationship between **the Eucharist, the bishop, and the unity of the Church**. For Ignatius, these were not separate concerns. Rather, they were **deeply interwoven realities**: the Church is one because the Eucharist is one, and the Eucharist is one because it is celebrated under the bishop, who preserves apostolic teaching and communion.

The Eucharist and Ecclesial Unity:

St. Ignatius emphasizes repeatedly that the Eucharist is the **visible and spiritual center of Christian unity**. He exhorts the faithful in Philadelphia:

> "Take care, then, to participate in one Eucharist; for there is one flesh of our Lord Jesus Christ, and one cup that leads to unity in His blood; one altar, just as there is one bishop, along with the presbyters and deacons" (Letter to the Philadelphians, 4).

This sentence is profoundly theological. Ignatius affirms that there is **"one flesh"** of the Lord, echoing the language of the Incarnation and the Eucharist (John 1:14; John 6:51–56). He connects this "one flesh" to the **one cup**, the shared chalice that unites the faithful in the blood of Christ. These are not metaphors but sacramental realities. And he roots these Eucharistic elements in the **unity of the altar**, which must be presided over by the bishop, together with the ordained presbyters and deacons.

In this vision, the Eucharist is the **sacrament of ecclesial communion**, and the bishop is its visible guarantee. To participate in the Eucharist is to participate in the Church. And to separate from the bishop is to separate from the one altar, the one cup, and ultimately the one Body of Christ.

The Role of the Bishop in Eucharistic Unity:

St. Ignatius is not primarily concerned with hierarchical authority for its own sake. Rather, he understands that the bishop is the **link to the apostolic foundation** of the Church. The bishop represents both the unity of the local church and its communion with the universal Church. He is the **guardian of true doctrine** and the **presider over the Eucharist**, which is the source and summit of the Church's life.

> "Let no one do anything of concern to the Church without the bishop. Let that be considered a valid Eucharist which is celebrated under the bishop or one to whom he has committed it" (Letter to the Smyrnaeans, 8).

This statement highlights the theological seriousness of Eucharistic unity. A Eucharist celebrated apart from the bishop is not merely unauthorized — it is **invalid** because it contradicts the visible and spiritual unity that Christ intended for His Body. The bishop is not a bureaucratic overseer but the **liturgical and apostolic center of unity**, a living continuation of the apostolic circle to whom Christ entrusted His authority.

Therefore, for Ignatius, **ecclesial schism and Eucharistic separation are the same sin**. To break away from the bishop is to break away from the Church. And to break away from the Eucharist is to break away from Christ Himself. The Eucharist is not an isolated event — it is the living bond that holds the Body of Christ together.

The Eucharist as the Medicine of Immortality:

St. Ignatius' understanding of the Eucharist is deeply sacramental and incarnational. He does not shy away from affirming the **Real Presence** of Christ in the Eucharistic elements. He boldly proclaims:

> "The Eucharist is the flesh of our Savior Jesus Christ, which suffered for our sins and which the Father, in His goodness, raised up again" (Letter to the Smyrnaeans, 7).

For St. Ignatius, the Eucharist is the very Body of the crucified and risen Lord — **the same flesh that was nailed to the Cross, the same flesh that emerged from the tomb**. It is not a symbol nor a mere memorial but the true and life-giving presence of the Incarnate Word. He calls it the **"medicine of immortality, the antidote against death, and the food that makes us live forever in Jesus Christ"** (*Letter to the Ephesians*, 20).

This Eucharistic realism is not meant to provoke theological debate—it is meant to **deepen the faith of believers** and bind them more closely to Christ and one another. It is through this sacrament that the Church is healed, nourished, and made one.

A Witness for the Divided Church Today:

St. Ignatius' vision of Eucharistic and ecclesial unity remains strikingly relevant today. In an era when Christians are divided into numerous denominations, each with their own altars and conflicting teachings, the clarity of his witness challenges us to reconsider the cost of our divisions.

He reminds us that the **Eucharist is not merely about private devotion or personal encounter with Christ**—it is about visible, tangible unity. It demands fidelity to the apostolic faith, communion with the legitimate bishop, and mutual love among all members of the Church.

> "Where the bishop is, there is the Church" (Letter to the Smyrnaeans, 8).

This short but powerful maxim encapsulates his entire ecclesiology. The Church is not an abstract idea or a loose association of believers—it is a Eucharistic communion under apostolic leadership. To find the true Church, one must find the Eucharist. And to find the Eucharist, one must be in communion with the bishop.

In St. Ignatius, we find not only a theological framework but also a pastoral heart—a man willing to suffer martyrdom rather than compromise the unity of the Church. His letters continue to speak prophetically to a fractured Christian world, urging us to return to the one altar, the one Eucharist, and the one Body of Christ.

4. The Eucharist as the Center of Unity in the Undivided Church

In the earliest centuries of Christianity, the Church existed as a **visible communion**, bound together by one faith, one baptism, and one table—the Eucharist. The idea of **multiple Eucharistic altars, divided by doctrine or hierarchy**, would have been unthinkable to early Christians. To partake in the Eucharist was not simply to receive Christ—it was to **confess one Church**, to **belong to one Body**, and to live in harmony with all those who shared in the same sacrament.

The Eucharist, therefore, was not an element of Christian life among many; it was the **center**—the axis around which the Church's worship, theology, and unity revolved. Christians recognized that **Eucharistic communion was ecclesial communion**. To receive the Eucharist from the altar of the Church was to **affirm one's full participation in the one, holy, catholic, and apostolic Church**. Conversely, to break from Eucharistic fellowship was to step outside the life of the Church itself.

One Altar, One Church, One Body:

The early Church saw no need for qualifying terms such as "Roman," "Eastern," or "Protestant." There was simply **the Church**, gathered around **the one altar**, proclaiming **the one Gospel**, and nourished by **the one Eucharist**. Though the Church was geographically dispersed across the Roman Empire and beyond, the liturgy, sacraments, apostolic tradition, and Eucharistic theology formed a consistent and united identity.

This unity was both **visible and sacramental**. It was safeguarded by apostolic succession, preserved through the common celebration of the Eucharist, and witnessed in the lives of the saints and martyrs. Christians of the second and third centuries could travel from one city to another and find themselves **at home in the liturgy**, recognizing the same prayers, structure, and reverence surrounding the Body and Blood of Christ.

To refuse Eucharistic unity—by rejecting the authority of the bishop, departing from the apostolic faith, or harboring unrepentant division—was to **separate oneself from the life-giving heart of the Church**. The Church Fathers were unequivocal on this point: there is no true Eucharist apart from the unity of the Church, and there is no true Church apart from the Eucharist.

Eucharistic Unity and the Nicene Creed:

By the time of the **First Ecumenical Council at Nicaea in 325 AD**, the Church's identity was formally expressed in the words that have shaped Christian confession for centuries:

> "I believe in one, holy, catholic, and apostolic Church."

These four marks were not abstract ideals—they were grounded in the **Eucharistic life** of the Church.

1- **One** – because the Eucharist unites all believers in Christ's one Body (1 Corinthians 10:17). In every liturgy, the Church proclaims and enacts her unity, not merely in word but in sacrament.

2- **Holy** – because Christ, truly present in the Eucharist, sanctifies His people. The Eucharist is the holy gift of the Holy One, imparting divine life to the faithful.

3- **Catholic** – because the Eucharist is celebrated universally, in every place and among every people, as the same unchanging mystery. It transcends culture and language, making the Church truly universal.

4- **Apostolic** – because the Eucharist is offered through bishops and priests ordained in apostolic succession. It is the sacrament of the faith that was once delivered to the saints and handed down through the laying on of hands.

Thus, the Nicene Creed does not merely describe the Church—it describes the **Eucharistic Church**, which is visibly united, spiritually sanctified, universally extended, and faithfully apostolic.

The Loss of Eucharistic Unity in Later Centuries:

Tragically, throughout Christian history, the unity once embodied in the Eucharist began to **fracture**. Theological disputes, cultural tensions, and political pressures led to a series of schisms, each one leaving behind **divided altars** and **separated communions**.

1- The **Council of Chalcedon (451 AD)**, though convened to clarify Christological doctrine, resulted in a major rift between the **Eastern Orthodox** and **Oriental Orthodox** Churches—a division that persists to this day despite sharing many elements of liturgical and sacramental life.

2- The **Great Schism of 1054**, the formal rupture between the **Eastern Orthodox Church** and the **Roman Catholic Church**, was rooted in long-standing theological and ecclesiological differences, particularly regarding papal primacy and the Filioque clause.

3- The **Protestant Reformation (16th century)** further fragmented the Western Church, introducing divergent doctrines about the Eucharist itself—ranging from real presence to symbolic memorial—and multiplying distinct ecclesial bodies, many of which have since lost sacramental continuity with the apostolic tradition.

Each of these breaks in communion was not merely administrative—it was **Eucharistic**. The one altar became many. The one cup was replaced with conflicting interpretations. And the visible sign of unity that Christ instituted became, for many, a source of division.

The Eucharist as the Key to Restoring Unity:

Despite these historical wounds, the Eucharist remains the **key to Christian unity**. As the early Church gathered around one table, so too must any authentic path to reconciliation be **grounded on the Eucharist**. Doctrinal dialogues and ecumenical gestures are essential, but they find their fulfillment only when Christians can once more stand together at the same altar, receive the same Body and Blood, and confess the same faith.

The Eucharist is not only the expression of unity—it is the **source and goal** of unity. Christ did not offer different bodies for different communities. He gave **one Body** and poured out **one Blood**, calling His people to be **one as He and the Father are one** (John 17:21). The visible unity of the Church will be restored when divided Christians no longer approach separate tables but once again gather as one family around the Eucharistic banquet.

As St. Paul reminds us:

> "Because there is one bread, we who are many are one body, for we all partake of the one bread" (1 Corinthians 10:17).

This Eucharistic truth still holds. It calls each generation to strive for that unity which the early Church knew and cherished—a unity not imposed but born of the Spirit, centered on the altar, and made manifest in the breaking of the Bread.

Conclusion

The testimony of the early Church resounds with a single, clear truth: the **Eucharist was the heart of Christian unity**. From the upper room in Jerusalem to the house churches of Antioch, from the pastoral letters of St. Ignatius to the ancient prayers of the *Didache*, the Church gathered as one Body around one altar to receive the one Lord.

The Eucharist was not a ritual accessory to the life of the Church—it **was** the life of the Church. It was through the breaking of the bread that Christ was made present, not only on the altar but in the hearts and relationships of His people. In the Eucharist, strangers became brothers, divisions were healed, and the Church revealed her truest identity: a people gathered into the unity of the Father through the Son by the power of the Holy Spirit.

This unity was not abstract. It was real, visible, and sacramental. The early believers understood that to participate in the Eucharist was to be **fully joined to Christ and one another**. To separate from the common table was to separate from the Church. Eucharistic communion and ecclesial communion were inseparable, and both were entrusted to the care of the bishop, who, standing at the altar, became the visible sign of Christ's presence and the continuity of apostolic faith.

Over time, this unity would be tested and fractured. Doctrinal conflicts, ecclesiastical rivalries, and political ambitions led to tragic schisms—dividing Christians not only in name but at the very table of the Lord. The one altar became many, the one cup fragmented, and the very sacrament of unity became a mirror reflecting disunity.

Yet the Eucharist has never lost its power. It remains today, as it was in the beginning, the **source and summit** of the Church's life. It is the place where Christ gives Himself wholly, calling His people to be one as He and the Father are one (John 17:21). It is the table that heals, gathers, and sends. And it is the mystery through which the Church is continually made new.

To seek Christian unity, then, is to return to the Eucharist—not merely as a doctrine but as a divine gift that calls for humility, repentance, reconciliation, and love. The Eucharist reminds us that unity is not something we create but something we receive. It is not imposed but **revealed** in Christ, who gives us His Body so that we may become His Body.

As we reflect on the witness of the early Church, we are called to rediscover the Eucharist as the **unifying reality** of the Christian life. If we long for unity today — as families, parishes, denominations, and nations — we must look again to the table where Christ is present, where His Body is offered, and where His people are made one.

> "Because there is one bread, we who are many are one body, for we all partake of the one bread" (1 Corinthians 10:17).

May this enduring truth guide our hearts and shape our communities as we journey together toward the fullness of unity in Christ.

Chapter 5

Historical Schisms and the Church Unity

From the beginning, the Eucharist has been the sacrament of **unity** — the holy mystery through which believers are united with Christ and with one another as **one body**. It is the table at which all distinctions dissolve: Jew and Gentile, male and female, rich and poor — all are made equal in Christ, nourished through His Body and Blood, and bound together by the Holy Spirit. As the Apostle Paul proclaimed, "Because there is one bread, we who are many are one body; for we all partake of the one bread" (1 Corinthians 10:17).

Yet, while the Eucharist reveals and creates unity, **history tells a different story** — a story marked by division, schism, and separation. Though the Lord Jesus fervently prayed, "That they may all be one… so that the world may believe that You sent Me" (John 17:21), the visible unity of His Church has been repeatedly broken. And at the heart of every major division in Church history lies a tragic consequence: the **fracturing of Eucharistic communion**.

This chapter explores the **wounds of division** that have afflicted the Body of Christ, focusing specifically on the historical moments that led to **separation at the Eucharistic table**. These divisions were often rooted in theological disputes, political tensions, and cultural misunderstandings — but their deepest impact has been **sacramental**. When communion with one another was lost, so too was communion in the Eucharist. The one Body became fragmented, and Christians who once shared the same Bread began to worship at separate altars.

Our goal is not to recount these schisms merely as historical facts but to understand their **theological and ecclesial significance** and to discern the path toward **reconciliation and restoration**. For if the Eucharist is truly the sign and source of Christian unity, then healing these divisions must begin at the altar.

In this chapter, we will examine four key events that shaped the landscape of Christian division:

1- The **Council of Chalcedon (451 AD)** and the resulting separation between the Eastern and Oriental Orthodox Churches—one of the earliest schisms that fractured communion despite shared reverence for Christ.

2- The **Great Schism (1054 AD)** between Eastern Orthodoxy and Roman Catholicism—rooted in disputes over theology, papal primacy, and liturgical differences.

3- The **Protestant Reformation (16th century)**—a movement that sought to reform abuses but ultimately introduced divergent interpretations of the Eucharist, leading to further fragmentation.

4- The **ongoing impact** of these historical breaks on modern Eucharistic practice—and the hopeful steps taken toward dialogue, mutual recognition, and healing.

As we walk through these pivotal moments, we are invited to reflect not only on the causes of separation but on the **urgency of restoring Eucharistic unity**. Unity at the table is not a luxury for the Church—it is the very **expression of her**

identity. To be Church is to be one Body, nourished by one Eucharist, gathered around one altar.

This chapter does not seek to assign blame or rekindle old hostilities. Rather, it seeks to foster **understanding**, **honesty**, and **hope** — hope that the Church, wounded though she may be, can rediscover the unity she once knew by returning to the **Eucharist as her center and her peace**.

For if we share the same Lord, the same baptism, and the same Spirit, then we must also seek the grace to once again share **the same table**.

"Is Christ divided?" (1 Corinthians 1:13)

Let this question stir our hearts as we begin this reflection — and let the longing for Eucharistic unity lead us toward reconciliation and renewal.

1. The Major Divisions in Church History and Their Impact on Eucharistic Fellowship

In the earliest centuries of the Christian faith, the Church was visibly and spiritually united. Believers from diverse regions gathered as **one body**, sharing in **one faith**, celebrating the **same sacraments**, and partaking of the **one Eucharist** around the **one altar**. This unity was sustained through fidelity to apostolic teaching, the guidance of bishops in apostolic succession, and the shared liturgical and sacramental life of the universal Church. The Eucharist — celebrated in the breaking of the bread — was not merely a sacred rite; it was the **very center of communion**, the sacrament of unity in Christ.

As the Apostle Paul declared to the Corinthian Church:

"For also by one Spirit we were all baptized into one body, whether Jews or Greeks, whether slaves or free, and we were all made to drink of one Spirit" (1 Corinthians 12:13).

This profound vision of the Church as one body—formed by one Spirit and sustained by one Eucharist—guided the early Christian imagination. The Eucharist was both the **expression** and the **cause** of that unity. To receive the Body and Blood of Christ was to proclaim oneself a member of His Body, the Church. To share in the one chalice was to be bound in love not only to Christ but to every fellow believer who knelt at the same altar.

The Tragedy of Division:

However, as the centuries passed, this unity began to strain under the weight of **doctrinal disagreements**, **ecclesial conflicts**, **cultural misunderstandings**, and **political interference**. These tensions—some theological in nature, others rooted in language, liturgical expression, or imperial power—led to tragic schisms. At first, they seemed manageable. But over time, they deepened into full-scale separations that would fracture the Body of Christ and **divide the Eucharistic table**.

Each major division in Church history—whether at Chalcedon in 451, Constantinople in 1054, or Wittenberg in 1517—has left a lasting mark on the Church. What had once been one altar became many. What had once been a single communion became a series of **separate ecclesial identities**, each with its own understanding of the Eucharist and, often, its own restrictions on who could partake of it. The visible sign of unity — **the one Bread and the one Cup** — was no longer universally shared.

Fragmentation of Eucharistic Fellowship:

The result of these divisions was not merely theological divergence or institutional separation. The deepest wound was **Eucharistic estrangement**. Christians who once stood together at the same altar, confessing the same creed and receiving the same Lord, now found themselves **excluded from one another's tables**. Where there had once been a common chalice, now there are boundaries and barriers. Where there had been shared worship, now there is separation and silence.

This fragmentation of Eucharistic fellowship contradicts the very nature of the Eucharist. The sacrament of the altar is not merely about personal communion with God — it is about **communal union with the Body of Christ**, the Church. To break that communion is to weaken the witness of the Church and obscure the Gospel's message of reconciliation.

St. Paul, addressing a divided Corinthian church, asked the piercing question:

"Is Christ divided?" (1 Corinthians 1:13)

This rhetorical challenge resounds through the centuries. If Christ is one — and if we all share in His one Body — how can we remain **divided at His table**?

The question is not merely theoretical. It strikes at the heart of Christian identity and Eucharistic theology. For the early Church, to break the unity of the Eucharist was to break the unity of the Church. And conversely, to seek the healing of the

Church's wounds must begin with a return to the **one Bread and one Cup**, offered for the life of the world.

A Call to Self-Examination:

Each division in Church history invites us to **self-examination**. Were the causes purely theological, or were they also human—marked by pride, misunderstanding, fear, and political ambition? And more importantly, are we willing today to listen, to dialogue, and to seek reconciliation, not by watering down the truth, but by recovering the Eucharist as the **place of encounter**, the **sign of charity**, and the **source of unity**?

The loss of Eucharistic fellowship is one of the Church's deepest wounds. But it is not beyond healing. The same Holy Spirit who united the Church at Pentecost still works within her today, calling the faithful to repentance, humility, and renewed love for one another.

As we examine the particular historical events that led to these divisions—the Council of Chalcedon, the Great Schism, and the Protestant Reformation—we must do so with a spirit not of judgment but of **hope**. For the Eucharist not only reveals the divisions of the Church—it also holds the promise of her **reunion**.

May the prayer of Christ echo in our hearts as we consider these events:

"That they may all be one; even as You, Father, are in Me and I in You, that they also may be in Us, so that the world may believe that You sent Me" (John 17:21).

2. The Council of Chalcedon (451) and the Separation Between Eastern and Oriental Orthodox

Among the earliest and most enduring divisions in the history of the Church is the separation that followed the **Council of Chalcedon** in 451 AD. This division created two major streams of Eastern Christianity:

1. **The Chalcedonian Churches**, which include the Eastern Orthodox Church, the Roman Catholic Church, and later the Protestant churches.

2. **The Non-Chalcedonian or Oriental Orthodox Churches**, which include the Coptic Orthodox Church of Egypt, the Armenian Apostolic Church, the Syriac Orthodox Church, the Ethiopian and Eritrean Orthodox Churches, and the Malankara (Indian) Orthodox Church.

This break, often called the **first great schism** of the Church, did not arise from a rejection of Christ or the Gospel but from a profound theological dispute over how best to articulate the mystery of **Christ's nature**.

The Christological Dispute:

The central question debated at Chalcedon was this: **How do we describe the relationship between Christ's divinity and His humanity?**

The Council of Chalcedon sought to clarify the faith by affirming that Christ is:

> "One and the same Son... perfect in divinity and perfect in humanity, truly God and truly man... acknowledged in two natures without confusion, without change, without division, and without separation."

This Chalcedonian Definition emphasized that Christ's two natures—divine and human—are fully united in one Person, without mixing or blending, without separation or division. It was meant as a careful balance, protecting against both Nestorianism (which over-separated the natures) and Eutychianism (which blurred them into one).

However, many Eastern Churches, especially in Egypt, Syria, and Armenia, feared that the Chalcedonian language risked **dividing Christ into two persons** or diminishing the unity of His incarnation. They preferred the Christology of **St. Cyril of Alexandria**, who spoke of Christ as having **"one incarnate nature of God the Word"** (*mia physis tou Theou Logou sesarkōmenē*)—a formula that emphasized the complete union of divinity and humanity in the single Person of Christ.

Although both groups sought to defend the mystery of Christ's incarnation, differences in theological emphasis, language, and political pressures led to misunderstanding, mistrust, and, ultimately, schism.

The Consequences for Eucharistic Communion:

The fallout from Chalcedon was not merely a theoretical debate—it had **profound ecclesial and sacramental consequences**.

1- Separate hierarchies were established. The Chalcedonian and Non-Chalcedonian Churches no longer recognized one another's bishops or councils.

2- Eucharistic communion was broken. What had once been one Church, sharing the same altar, became two distinct communions, each with its own liturgical traditions and sacramental discipline.

3- Over time, centuries of isolation hardened initial misunderstandings, creating the impression that the two families of Churches had irreconcilable Christology.

Yet, beneath the surface, something remarkable remained: **both sides continued to profess the same core faith in Christ**. Despite their divergent theological expressions, they both believed in the true divinity and true humanity of the Lord, and they both preserved the apostolic faith, sacraments, and apostolic succession.

Steps Toward Reconciliation:

In the modern era, particularly in the second half of the twentieth century, new efforts at theological dialogue have shed light on the nature of this ancient division. Joint Christological statements between the Chalcedonian (Eastern Orthodox and Catholic) and Non-Chalcedonian (Oriental Orthodox) Churches have revealed that much of the division was rooted **more in terminology and historical misunderstanding than in real theological disagreement**.

For example, in 1989, a Joint Statement between the Coptic Orthodox Church and the Eastern Orthodox Church declared:

> "We have inherited from our fathers the same authentic Orthodox Christological faith, despite the differences in terminology and interpretation which arose between the two families of Churches."

In several local contexts, bishops from both communions have begun **opening their altars to one another** under specific conditions, restoring partial Eucharistic sharing as a sign of growing unity. While full reconciliation has not yet been achieved, these dialogues represent a significant step forward, offering hope that the wound of Chalcedon may one day be healed.

The Eucharistic Implication:

The separation caused by Chalcedon serves as a poignant reminder that **theological clarity matters**, but so too do humility, patience, and love. To preserve Eucharistic unity, we must be willing to listen deeply, engage honestly, and work tirelessly to overcome misunderstandings.

St. Cyril of Alexandria, whose teaching played such a pivotal role in this controversy, offers a beautiful vision of the Eucharistic mystery that unites all believers:

> "One body was offered for all, and through this one body, we are all united in one Spirit"(Commentary on John 6:56).

If we confess the same Christ—if we partake of His one Body and drink from His one Cup—how can we remain separated at His Table?

A Lesson for Today:

The division between the Eastern and Oriental Orthodox Churches stands as one of the oldest wounds in Christian history, yet it also offers one of the **greatest opportunities for healing**. Unlike many later divisions, which involved sharper doctrinal disputes, the Chalcedonian schism reveals the power of dialogue to uncover shared faith beneath layers of historical and linguistic difference.

For today's Church, the lesson is clear: the path to Eucharistic reconciliation requires pastoral sensitivity, mutual respect, and a shared longing for the unity that Christ prayed for. Only when we commit ourselves to this patient and loving work can we hope to restore the visible communion that was broken so many centuries ago.

3. The Great Schism (1054): The Divide Between East and West

The year 1054 stands as one of the most significant—and sorrowful—moments in the history of the Church. Known as the **Great Schism**, this event marked the formal rupture between the **Eastern Orthodox Church** and the **Roman Catholic Church**, a division that has shaped the landscape of global Christianity ever since.

Before the schism, East and West shared not only the same apostolic faith but also **full Eucharistic communion**. Bishops and faithful traveled between Rome and Constantinople; liturgical traditions, though distinct in language and style, were recognized as authentically Christian, and the one Body of Christ was visibly present across the empire. Yet beneath this surface, unity, deep **theological, political, and cultural tensions** had been simmering for centuries.

Historical Context of the Schism:

The Eastern Church, centered in Constantinople, developed within the Greek-speaking world, shaped by the legacy of the Eastern Roman (Byzantine) Empire. The Western Church, centered in Rome, evolved within the Latin-speaking world, grappling with the collapse of the Western Roman Empire and the rise of new political powers. Over time, differences emerged—not only in language, liturgical expression, and administrative customs but also in theological formulation and ecclesiastical governance.

Though previous disagreements had strained relations, the events of 1054 formalized the split when the legates of Pope Leo IX excommunicated Patriarch Michael Cerularius of Constantinople, and the Patriarch responded by excommunicating the Pope and his legates. What had been a tense but unbroken communion became a hardened division.

Two central theological issues fueled the separation:

The Filioque Controversy:

Originally, the **Nicene-Constantinopolitan Creed** (381 AD) proclaimed that the **Holy Spirit proceeds from the Father** (John 15:26). Without an ecumenical council, however, the Western Church gradually added the phrase **"and the Son" (Latin:** *Filioque*) to the Creed, asserting that the Spirit proceeds from both the Father **and** the Son.

The Eastern Church objected to this addition—not only because it altered the original ecumenical Creed without universal consent but because it raised concerns about the inner life of the Trinity and the Father's unique role as the sole source (*archē*) within the Godhead. For the East, this change risked upsetting the delicate balance of Trinitarian theology; for the West, it was a legitimate clarification against Arianism.

The Papal Authority:

The West, particularly after the fall of the Western Roman Empire, came to emphasize the **universal primacy and jurisdiction** of the Bishop of Rome, seeing the Pope as the supreme earthly head of the Church. The East, while honoring the Pope as the "first among equals" (*primus inter pares*) among the patriarchs, rejected any notion of absolute or unilateral papal authority over the universal Church.

This dispute over governance and authority would become a central dividing line, with both sides unable to reconcile their differing ecclesiology.

The Consequences for Eucharistic Unity:

The tragedy of the Great Schism was not merely political or theoretical—it was profoundly **sacramental**.

Before the schism, East and West shared the **same Eucharist**, recognizing one another's sacraments, clergy, and liturgical life. After the schism, Eucharistic communion was **severed**. While the core of the faith remained remarkably similar, the inability to resolve theological and jurisdictional disputes resulted in mutual exclusion from the altar. Over the centuries, the two Churches developed distinct liturgical traditions, spiritual emphases, and theological languages.

The formal mutual excommunications—the symbolic seal of division—remained in place for over 900 years until they were **lifted in 1965** by **Pope St. Paul VI** and **Patriarch Athenagoras** during a historic meeting in Jerusalem. This was a monumental gesture of goodwill, signaling a desire for renewed dialogue and mutual respect, but it did not by itself restore Eucharistic communion.

Efforts Toward Reconciliation:

In the decades following the lifting of the excommunications, Catholic-Orthodox dialogue has made **significant progress**. Joint theological commissions have worked through many areas of common faith, clarifying misunderstandings and identifying genuine points of agreement.

However, full Eucharistic communion remains **unachieved**. Challenges persist, particularly concerning the nature of papal primacy, the relationship between local Churches and universal governance, and the healing of historical wounds. Yet the commitment to dialogue, the warm relations between many bishops and theologians, and the mutual recognition of shared sacramental life offer hope for the future.

A Eucharistic Foundation for Reconciliation:

The Eucharist stands at the heart of the longing for reconciliation between East and West. As St. John Chrysostom, the great preacher of Constantinople, once preached:

> "You cannot pray to the Father if you are divided from your brother. For it is one body that we partake of, and one table that we approach" (Homily on Matthew 5:23).

St. Chrysostom's words ring as true today as they did in the fourth century. The Eucharist is not simply a personal or local reality; it is the **universal sign of unity** in Christ. To approach the one altar while remaining divided from one another is to contradict the very nature of the sacrament.

The path toward restored communion between Catholic and Orthodox believers cannot be one of compromise or mere political agreement. It must be a journey rooted in truth, humility, and charity, seeking to restore the unity that flows from the one Bread and one Cup.

A Call to Hope:

Though nearly a thousand years of separation weigh heavily on the Christian conscience, we must remember that unity is not ultimately our achievement but **God's gift**. Christ Himself prayed for the unity of His followers, and the Holy Spirit continues to stir hearts, heal divisions, and guide the Church toward reconciliation.

As we reflect on the Great Schism, we are invited to pray, to hope, and to work for the day when East and West may once again gather at the same Eucharistic table—not as divided siblings, but as one family in Christ.

4. The Protestant Reformation and the Loss of a Unified Eucharistic Table

The **Protestant Reformation of the 16th century** stands as one of the most transformative—and most fragmenting—moments in the history of Western Christianity. What began as a movement to reform moral abuses and theological excesses within the Roman Catholic Church soon evolved into a deep theological, liturgical, and ecclesial rupture that reshaped the Christian world.

Among the many areas affected by the Reformation, perhaps none was more deeply impacted—or more central to the division—than the understanding of the **Eucharist**.

For over a millennium, Christians in both East and West had shared a common sacramental life centered on the belief in the **real presence** of Christ in the Eucharist. Although subtle theological differences existed, the core conviction remained: the bread and wine, through the consecration of the priest, became the true Body and Blood of the Lord, a mystery to be adored and received in faith.

The Reformation challenged this consensus, introducing **new interpretations** of the Lord's Supper and thereby fracturing the unified Eucharistic table that had once defined Christian life in the West.

The Reformers and Their Critique:

Key figures of the Reformation—such as **Martin Luther**, **Ulrich Zwingli**, and **John Calvin**—sought to correct what they saw as abuses in the Catholic Church, including the selling of indulgences, the corruption of church leadership, and the perceived overelaboration of sacramental theology.

While the Reformers agreed on many critiques, they quickly diverged in their understanding of the Eucharist:

1- **Lutheranism (Consubstantiation)**: Martin Luther firmly rejected the Catholic doctrine of **transubstantiation**, which taught that the substance of the bread and wine becomes the substance of Christ's Body and Blood. Yet Luther fiercely defended the **real presence** of Christ in the Eucharist. His view, often called **consubstantiation**, holds that Christ is truly present "in, with, and under" the bread and wine, which remain physically bread and wine. For Luther, the Eucharist was more than a symbol — it was a means of grace, the real gift of Christ's body for the forgiveness of sins.

2- **Calvinism (Spiritual Presence)**: John Calvin rejected both transubstantiation and consubstantiation, teaching instead that the Eucharist is a **spiritual participation** in Christ. According to Calvin, believers, by the power of the Holy Spirit and through faith, are lifted up to commune with the risen Christ, who remains in heaven. While rejecting a physical or material presence, Calvin still maintained that the Eucharist is a true means of grace and a profound spiritual mystery.

3- **Zwinglianism (Memorialism)**: Ulrich Zwingli took a more radical position, interpreting the Lord's Supper as a **symbolic remembrance** of Christ's death. For Zwingli, the bread and wine are memorials that direct the faithful to reflect on Christ's sacrifice, but they do not convey Christ's real presence or serve as a sacramental means of grace.

The Consequences for Eucharistic Communion:

These theological disagreements had enormous consequences for the unity of the Church. While Protestants agreed on the need for reform, their divergent Eucharistic theologies led to **internal fractures** within the Reformation itself. Lutheran, Reformed, and Radical Protestant communities emerged, each with its own liturgical practices, sacramental theology, and understanding of Christian worship.

In rejecting the Catholic and Orthodox understanding of the Eucharist as the sacramental real presence of Christ, many Protestant communities also **moved away from weekly Eucharistic celebration**, shifting the center of their worship from the altar to the pulpit. Preaching and the exposition of Scripture became the primary focus, while the Lord's Supper was often celebrated monthly, quarterly, or even less frequently.

Moreover, the **fragmentation of Protestant denominations** led to inconsistent Eucharistic practices across the Reformation landscape. In many cases, denominations refused to recognize one another's Eucharist, reflecting not only theological division but also a deep ecclesial and sacramental rupture.

A Loss of a Common Table:

For the early Church Fathers, the Eucharist was the heart of Christian unity. As **St. Irenaeus of Lyons** wrote in the second century:

> "Our way of thinking is in harmony with the Eucharist, and the Eucharist, in turn, confirms our way of thinking" (Against Heresies 4:18:5).

The loss of a common understanding of the Eucharist has thus become one of the greatest obstacles to restoring Christian unity. Without agreement on what the Eucharist is, it is difficult—if not impossible—for Christians of different traditions to share in Eucharistic communion. The body is divided where the table is divided.

A Challenge and an Invitation:

The Protestant Reformation raised important and necessary questions about ecclesial reform, the authority of Scripture, and the nature of grace. Yet, it also left behind deep wounds, particularly concerning sacramental life. Today, the challenge before Christians is to engage in honest dialogue, seeking not only to clarify doctrinal differences but also to rediscover the **unifying power of the Eucharist**.

Without a shared understanding of the Eucharist, Christian unity remains elusive. But with patient theological engagement, mutual respect, and the guidance of the Holy Spirit, the divisions that once seemed insurmountable may yet be healed.

The Eucharist is not merely a doctrine or ritual—it is the **gift of Christ Himself**, given for the life of the world, and the place where the Church becomes most fully what she is:

> "Because there is one bread, we who are many are one body, for we all partake of the one bread"(1 Corinthians 10:17).

Let us remember that at the heart of Christian unity lies the Lord's Table, where He gives His Body and Blood so that His people may be one.

Conclusion: The Call to Restore Eucharistic Unity

The history we have traced in this chapter is a history marked by both **sorrow** and **hope**. On the one hand, it is the story of the Church's painful divisions—the fractures that have broken the visible Body of Christ and torn believers away from one Eucharistic table into many. On the other hand, it is also the story of God's unceasing work by the Holy Spirit to draw His people back together, to heal wounds, and to fulfill the prayer of Christ for unity.

Every major division in Church history has had at its heart a **Eucharistic rupture**:

At the **Council of Chalcedon (451)**, Eastern Orthodox and Oriental Orthodox Christians, despite their shared love for Christ, became divided over the language of Christology—and this theological disagreement led not only to separate hierarchies but to the breaking of Eucharistic fellowship.

In the **Great Schism of 1054**, East and West, long growing apart through political, cultural, and theological differences, finally stood on opposite shores, no longer able to approach the same altar, even though they shared centuries of common faith and sacramental life.

The **Protestant Reformation of the 16th century**, though born from an authentic desire to purify the Church and renew her in holiness, ultimately led to the splintering of the Western Christian world, creating a host of divergent views on the nature of the Eucharist and fragmenting the very heart of Christian communion.

These divisions are not merely historical footnotes or relics of past controversies. They have shaped the living experience of Christianity across the centuries, and they continue to define the fragmented landscape of the Church today. But they are also **wounds that cry out for healing**.

If Christ is One, His Table Must Be One:

The Eucharist is not a symbol of unity that we create; it is the living sacrament of the unity that **Christ Himself gives**. In every celebration of the Eucharist, the Church proclaims the mystery that the one Christ offers Himself as one Bread, one Body, one Cup for the life of the world. The early Church knew no divided tables, no parallel altars, and no separate communions. For the first Christians, to share the Eucharist was to be one Church. To break Eucharistic communion was to break the bond of the Church itself.

And so, we are confronted today with a profound challenge:

If Christ is **one**, how can His Body remain **divided**? If the Eucharist is the place where we encounter the living Christ, how can we remain separated from one another at His Table?

The call to restore Eucharistic unity is not a call to theological compromise or institutional uniformity. It is a call to return to the **unity Christ desires** — the unity for which He prayed on the night before His Passion:

> "That they may all be one; even as You, Father, are in Me and I in You, that they also may be in Us, so that the world may believe that You sent Me" (John 17:21).

A Path of Dialogue, Love, and the Holy Spirit

The road to restored Eucharistic communion is neither easy nor short. Centuries of misunderstanding, hardened positions, and legitimate theological differences cannot be erased overnight. But the Spirit of God has not abandoned His Church. Across the world, Catholic, Orthodox, and Protestant theologians, pastors, and faithful are engaging in **honest dialogue**, seeking common ground, clarifying differences, and rediscovering the bonds that still unite us.

Restoring Eucharistic unity requires more than official agreements or signed documents. It demands **repentance**, **humility**, and **love** — a willingness to acknowledge past wrongs, to forgive old wounds, and to listen with open hearts to the voice of the Spirit. It calls us to recognize that unity is not an achievement we can manufacture but a **gift** we must receive, a gift already offered by Christ in the Eucharist.

The Eucharist as the Path to True Unity:

The Eucharist is not merely one path to unity among many. It is **the** path. For in the Eucharist, the Church does not simply proclaim unity; she enacts it. She becomes what she receives — the one Body of Christ, broken and given for the life of the world.

The Eucharist shows us the shape of true unity:

- A unity grounded in truth, not mere sentiment.

- A unity lived out in love, not imposed by power.

- A unity born of Christ's sacrifice, not human ambition.

The question before us, then, is not merely historical or theological. It is deeply spiritual and profoundly personal:

Will we follow the path of Eucharistic unity? Will we open our hearts to the healing work of the Spirit? Will we strive, in our own communities and lives, to make Christ's prayer for unity a living reality?

A Closing Invitation:

As we close this chapter, let us remember that the Eucharist is not just a doctrine to defend or a ritual to preserve. It is the living presence of Christ among His people, the gift of His Body and Blood, offered so that **we may be one**. Let us commit ourselves to the work of reconciliation, trusting that what seems impossible for us is possible for God.

The unity of the Church is not just for the Church's sake; it is, as Jesus prayed, **"so that the world may believe"** (John 17:21).

The Eucharist is the path to true unity. Will we follow it?

Chapter 6

The Tragedy of Eucharistic Separation

From the earliest days of the Christian Church, the Eucharist has stood at the center of Christian faith and practice. It is more than a ritual, more than a symbol, and more than a religious observance—it is the living, holy mystery through which Christ Himself unites believers to His life, His death, and His resurrection. The Eucharist is the sacrament of unity, a divine gift given by Christ to bind together His Body, the Church, in perfect communion.

Yet today, as we look across the Christian world, we are confronted with a heartbreaking and undeniable reality: the very table that was meant to unite the faithful has become a point of division, exclusion, and estrangement. Instead of gathering as one body to partake of the one bread and the one cup, Christian communities stand apart, separated by centuries of doctrinal disagreements, historical grievances, and ecclesial boundaries.

This chapter begins with a sobering acknowledgment: despite the shared confession of faith proclaimed each Sunday in the Nicene Creed—"I believe in one, holy, catholic, and apostolic Church"—the reality on the ground tells a different story. The Eucharistic separation between Orthodox, Catholic, and Protestant traditions exposes a visible contradiction between what the Church claims and what the Church lives. It is a tragedy not only because it wounds the Body of Christ but because it diminishes the Church's witness before the world.

Why has the Eucharist, the very sacrament meant to heal and reconcile, become the focal point of our divisions? Why do we treat the Lord's table as a reward for theological agreement rather than a gift of grace that calls us into deeper unity? Why do churches so often insist on resolving every doctrinal detail before gathering at the same altar when the earliest believers, though diverse in understanding, found their oneness precisely in breaking bread together?

In this chapter, we will explore the tragedy of Eucharistic separation by addressing four key themes:

1- The contradiction between affirming the one, holy, catholic, and apostolic Church and refusing Eucharistic unity.

2- The tension between doctrinal differences and Christ's command to love and be one.

3- The relationship between theological dialogues and Eucharistic unity—questioning which should come first.

4- The damaging impact of Christian division on the Church's evangelistic mission.

We will listen not only to the words of Scripture but also to the voices of the early Church Fathers, whose wisdom reminds us that the Eucharist is not merely an individual experience but a communal, ecclesial act. We will consider how the Church's disunity at the Eucharistic table weakens her witness to the world and undermines the very message of reconciliation she is called to proclaim.

Above all, this chapter calls us to consider the urgency of restoring Eucharistic communion—not as a sentimental longing for a bygone era but as a living, practical necessity for the Church's faithfulness to her Lord. Christ prayed that His followers would be one "so that the world may believe" (John 17:21). That oneness is not an abstract ideal; it is meant to be embodied at the Eucharistic table, where believers become one body by partaking of the one bread.

The Eucharist is the place where Christ's sacrificial love overcomes human division. It is the place where grace triumphs over legalism, where forgiveness heals wounds, and where unity becomes visible, tangible, and real. To continue separating ourselves at the Lord's table is not merely a matter of historical habit or ecclesial discipline—it is, at its heart, a tragedy that cuts against the very gospel we proclaim.

In the pages that follow, we invite you to reflect deeply, to pray earnestly, and to consider what it would mean for the Church to take seriously Christ's call to Eucharistic unity. For in answering that call, we do not merely solve an internal problem; we bear witness to the reconciling love of God before a watching world.

1. The Contradiction of Affirming "One, Holy, Catholic, and Apostolic Church" While Refusing Eucharistic Unity

One of the most profound declarations of Christian faith is found in the Nicene Creed, which has been recited in churches across centuries, cultures, and denominations. With clear, resounding voices, Christians proclaim together:

> "I believe in one, holy, catholic, and apostolic Church."

These words are not mere liturgical formalities; they embody the essential marks of the Church as confessed by the universal body of Christ. To say that the Church is **one** is to affirm its unity under Christ, its one Head. To say that it is **holy** is to affirm its sanctification by the Holy Spirit. To say that it is **catholic** is to declare its universality, embracing all believers across time and space. To say that it is **apostolic** is to affirm its foundation upon the teachings and witness of the apostles.

And yet—despite this bold, universal confession—the lived reality of the Church often reveals a tragic contradiction. Nowhere is this contradiction more visible and painful than at the Eucharistic table.

Though Christians affirm in word that they belong to one Church, they live in practice as if they are many. The Eucharist, which Christ instituted as the supreme sign and means of unity, has instead become the most visible dividing line among Christians. While we may join our voices in confessing the Nicene Creed, we part ways when it comes time to share the Body and Blood of Christ.

This raises unavoidable and uncomfortable questions:

- If the Church is one, why do different Christian traditions refuse to share the Eucharist?

- If the Eucharist is the sign of unity, why do Christians insist on achieving perfect unity before approaching communion?

- If Christ offered His Body and Blood for the life of the world, why do so many churches place barriers— whether doctrinal, historical, or disciplinary—around the Eucharistic table?

These are not rhetorical or merely academic questions; they strike at the very heart of what it means to be the Church of Jesus Christ.

The Early Church's Vision of Unity:

To understand the gravity of today's Eucharistic separation, we must look back to the early Church, where the Eucharist was understood not as the prize for unity achieved but as the very foundation of unity itself.

- In **Acts 2:42**, we read that the first believers "were continually devoting themselves to the apostles' teaching and to fellowship, to the breaking of bread and to prayer." The breaking of bread — the Eucharist — was central to the life of the Church, binding together those who had come to faith in Christ.

- In **1 Corinthians 10:16-17**, St. Paul reminds the Church that "the cup of blessing which we bless, is it not a sharing in the blood of Christ? The bread which we break, is it not a sharing in the body of Christ? Because there is one bread, we who are many are one body, for we all partake of the one bread." Here, the apostle points to the Eucharist not only as a symbol but as the enactment of the Church's unity.

- In **Ephesians 4:4-6**, Paul exhorts the believers, saying, "There is one body and one Spirit, just as you also were called in one hope of your calling; one Lord, one faith, one baptism, one God and Father of all who is over all and through all and in all." Unity, for Paul, is woven into the very fabric of the Church's existence.

Despite these biblical foundations, today's Christian communities often find themselves locked in a pattern of contradiction. They affirm shared creeds but deny shared communion. They profess one faith but maintain divided tables. They claim one baptism but enforce separate altars.

A Visible Wound and a Weak Witness:

This contradiction is not merely an internal issue for theologians and church leaders to ponder; it is a visible wound in the Body of Christ that weakens the Church's witness to the world. As Jesus Himself prayed in John 17:21, **"That they may all be one, just as You, Father, are in Me and I in You, so that the world may believe that You sent Me."** The unity of the Church is meant to be a living testimony to the reality of Christ's mission.

When the world looks at a fractured and divided Church, when it sees Christians refusing to share the Lord's Supper with one another, what message does it receive? Does it see the love of Christ? Does it see the power of the Gospel? Or does it see a house divided against itself, undermining the very message it claims to proclaim?

This section of the chapter invites the reader to grapple deeply with these tensions—not to dismiss them as unsolvable but to take seriously the call to reconciliation and restoration at the Eucharistic table. The contradiction between the Church's confession and its practice is not a minor matter; it is a spiritual crisis that demands urgent reflection, repentance, and action.

In the following pages, we will explore how this contradiction developed, why it continues, and what it will take for the Church to recover the unity that Christ prayed for and that the Eucharist so powerfully embodies.

2. Doctrinal Differences vs. the Command to Love and Be One in Christ

Across the history of the Church, few things have caused deeper wounds or more enduring divisions than doctrinal disagreements. From the early Christological controversies to the Great Schism between East and West, from the Protestant Reformation to modern denominational fragmentation, doctrinal disputes have marked the Christian landscape with division.

And yet, when we turn to the New Testament, we find a striking emphasis: the call to **love and unity** is placed above the pursuit of doctrinal perfection. While fidelity to the truth is essential, it is never presented as a justification for withholding love or breaking communion with one another. In fact, Scripture consistently warns against elevating knowledge over love and insists that true discipleship is measured not by theological precision but by the visible expression of love and unity among believers.

The Command of Christ: Love and Unity as the Mark of Discipleship:

At the heart of Jesus' teaching is not a demand for intellectual mastery or theological uniformity but a clear and uncompromising command to love:

> "A new commandment I give to you, that you love one another, even as I have loved you, that you also love one another. By this all will know that you are

> My disciples if you have love for one another" (John 13:34-35).

Love is not optional in the Christian life; it is the very evidence of authentic discipleship. Jesus' high priestly prayer in John 17 goes even further, expressing His deep longing that His followers would be united:

> "That they may all be one; even as You, Father, are in Me and I in You, that they also may be in Us, so that the world may believe that You sent Me" (John 17:21).

This unity is not merely a sentimental or spiritual feeling — it is meant to be real, tangible, and visible. It is a unity that the world can see and recognize as a sign that Jesus truly comes from the Father.

The Teaching of St. Paul: Unity Over Division

The apostle Paul, who tirelessly defended the truth of the Gospel, never wavered in his insistence that love and unity take precedence over divisions. In his famous passage on love, Paul writes:

> "And if I have the gift of prophecy and know all mysteries and all knowledge; and if I have all faith, so as to remove mountains, but do not have love, I am nothing" (1 Corinthians 13:2).

Knowledge, even theological knowledge, is empty without love. Paul calls believers to:

> "Make every effort to keep the unity of the Spirit in the bond of peace" (Ephesians 4:3).

And again:

> "Therefore, accept one another, just as Christ also accepted us, to the glory of God" (Romans 15:7).

For Paul, love and unity are not add-ons to the Christian life—they are its very essence. Without them, the Church's confession of faith becomes hollow.

Does Doctrine Justify Eucharistic Separation?

Of course, doctrine matters. The Church is called to uphold the truth of the faith, handed down from the apostles and guarded through the centuries. But here we must ask: **Is the Eucharist a prize for achieving doctrinal agreement, or is it the living presence of Christ given to draw His people together?**

There are several key points to consider:

1- The Eucharist is not a theological debate; it is **the real presence of Christ** given to His people for their salvation, sanctification, and communion.

2- The first disciples, even with different understandings and varying levels of maturity, **broke bread together** and found unity in the shared life of Christ (Acts 2:42).

3- Throughout His ministry, Christ welcomed sinners, tax collectors, and even doubters to His table—not because they were theologically perfect, but because He was calling them to Himself. Why, then, do churches today impose barriers of theological perfection that even Christ Himself did not demand?

The Wisdom of St. Augustine:

The early Church Father St. Augustine offers a profound insight into the relationship between the Eucharist and love:

> "Let us love Christ in the Eucharist, and let us love one another in Christ. For when we break one bread, we must not break the love that binds us" (Sermon 272).

St. Augustine reminds us that Eucharistic unity is not about perfect agreement on every point of doctrine; it is about the love that binds believers together in Christ. The Eucharist, after all, is not ours—it is the Lord's. It is He who invites; it is He who gives; it is He who unites.

To insist on absolute doctrinal conformity before sharing in the Eucharist is to misunderstand both the purpose of the sacrament and the nature of the Church. Eucharistic unity does not require the erasure of all differences, but it does require a heart of love, humility, and openness—a readiness to recognize the work of Christ in one another, even across lines of disagreement.

In the pages that follow, we will wrestle honestly with the challenge of doctrinal differences, but we will do so with the conviction that **love must come first**. For without love, no doctrine, however correct, can bring life. And without unity, no Eucharist, however beautifully celebrated, can bear full witness to the reconciling love of Christ.

3. Theological Dialogues vs. Eucharistic Unity: Which Should Come First?

For centuries, Christian leaders, theologians, and councils have approached the question of unity as a matter of doctrine first and communion second. The prevailing logic goes like this: **if churches are divided over theological disagreements, especially concerning the Eucharist, how can they possibly share the Eucharist together?** According to this reasoning, doctrinal clarity must precede Eucharistic sharing; reconciliation at the altar must wait until reconciliation in belief is complete.

We see this pattern repeated across church history. The Catholic and Orthodox Churches, though they share the ancient creeds, the sacraments, and apostolic succession, have been engaged in theological dialogues for nearly a millennium since the Great Schism—and yet, full Eucharistic communion remains elusive. Likewise, Protestant denominations, though often willing to cooperate in mission and social witness, continue to be divided over crucial questions about the nature of the Eucharist, its meaning, and its administration.

In this context, many Christians have accepted the idea that **doctrinal unity must always come first** and that Eucharistic unity can only follow as its final fruit. But is this the only possible path? And is it, in fact, the path that Christ Himself lays before His Church?

Jesus' Example: Fellowship Before Full Understanding:

When we look at the ministry of Jesus, we see a striking pattern: **fellowship often precedes understanding**. Christ did not wait for His disciples to achieve perfect comprehension before drawing them into table fellowship.

- He ate with sinners, tax collectors, and outcasts long before they understood the depth of His mission or repented of their sins.

- At the Last Supper, He shared the bread and cup with the very disciples who would soon betray, deny, or abandon Him.

- On the road to Emmaus, the two disciples only recognized the risen Christ **in the breaking of the bread** (Luke 24:30–31), not in the earlier conversation or theological explanation.

In every case, **the act of fellowship at the table opened the door to deeper revelation, not the other way around**. The Eucharist was not treated as the reward for doctrinal achievement but as the means by which Christ revealed Himself and drew His followers into communion.

The Eucharist as the Pathway to Unity:

This raises an urgent and challenging question for the Church today: **Could it be that Eucharistic unity itself is the path toward greater theological reconciliation rather than the final goal to be achieved only after all differences are resolved?**

- If Christians from divided traditions gathered regularly around the same altar, would that not open hearts to greater dialogue, mutual understanding, and reconciliation?

- If believers prayed together in the shared mystery of Christ's presence, might they not find their differences softened by the experience of God's grace?

- If the early Church did not demand perfect uniformity before breaking bread together, why do we impose such demands now?

The pattern of the early Church suggests that unity was **lived before it was fully understood**. The Eucharist was the visible sign of that unity, a shared participation in the one Body of Christ, even amidst diversity of thought and background.

The Wisdom of St. John Chrysostom:

St. John Chrysostom, the great preacher and teacher of the Church, warned against allowing divisions to fester at the very table of the Lord:

> "If we are divided at the Lord's Table, how can we be united in Christ? Let the table bring us together, for it is the table of love, not of division" (Homily on 1 Corinthians 24:4).

St. Chrysostom reminds us that the Eucharist is not merely a theological concept or a boundary marker—it is a table of love meant to draw God's people together into visible, embodied unity.

This section invites us to rethink the order of our priorities. **Rather than waiting for unity to be fully achieved before we come to the table, might we begin by coming to the table and trusting that Christ will accomplish the unity we cannot achieve on our own?** In the Eucharist, we encounter not only one another but the living presence of Christ Himself — the One who makes us one.

As we move forward, we must confront the uncomfortable reality that our divisions are often perpetuated not only by theological disagreements but also by fear, pride, and an unwillingness to take the risk of shared communion. The Eucharistic table calls us beyond these barriers, challenging us to trust in Christ's power to unite His Church, not by human effort alone, but through His grace made present among us.

4. The Witness of Christian Division and Its Impact on Evangelism

At the very heart of the Church's mission is the call to proclaim the good news of Jesus Christ to the world. Evangelism is not an optional activity for the Church; it is the natural outflow of her identity as the Body of Christ, sent into the world to bear witness to God's reconciling love. Yet one of the greatest and most persistent obstacles to this mission is the tragic disunity among Christians, particularly when it comes to the Eucharist.

The scandal of Christian division is not just a theological problem — it is a missional crisis. When non-Christians look at the Church and see fractured communities, divided denominations, competing claims, and above all, separated

Eucharistic tables, they are often left to wonder: **if Christians cannot love and reconcile with each other, why should we believe their message about the love and reconciliation of God?**

Jesus' Prayer for Unity as an Evangelistic Witness:

The Lord Jesus, in His high priestly prayer recorded in John 17, prays not only for His immediate disciples but for all who will believe through their word. At the center of His prayer is the plea for unity:

"I in them and You in Me, that they may be perfected in unity, so that the world may know that You sent Me, and loved them, even as You have loved Me" (John 17:23).

Jesus links the unity of His followers directly to the credibility of their witness before the world. In other words, Christian unity is not merely an internal matter; it has profound consequences for evangelism. A divided Church sends a divided message.

How Division Weakens Evangelism:

- If Christians cannot love one another, how can they convincingly call the world to the love of Christ? When believers are known more for their quarrels, splits, and mutual condemnations than for their shared love and fellowship, the gospel invitation loses its credibility.

- If every denomination maintains a separate Eucharist, marked by exclusive boundaries, how can the world believe that there is truly **one Christ**, one Gospel, one salvation offered to all? The fragmentation of the Eucharistic table sends the message that even within

Christianity, there is no agreement on the most central mystery of the faith.

- The lack of Eucharistic unity makes Christianity appear not as the universal, reconciling body of Christ but as a fractured and unconvincing collection of religious groups, each jealously guarding its own boundaries.

In a world already marked by suspicion, division, and mistrust, the Church is called to stand as a radiant sign of unity in diversity, of reconciliation across differences, and of a love that overcomes all barriers. When the Church fails to embody this unity, she weakens her evangelistic witness and clouds the face of Christ before a watching world.

The Urgency of Restoring Eucharistic Unity:

If the Church truly desires to reach the world with the Gospel, she must take seriously the call to restore unity at the Eucharistic table. This is not merely a matter of ecumenical politeness or institutional cooperation — it is a matter of fidelity to Christ's own desire for His Church and effectiveness in the mission He has entrusted to her.

To restore Eucharistic unity, we must:

- **Prioritize love over legalism.** While the Church must uphold truth, she must never allow legalistic boundaries to override the command to love and the call to unity.

- **See the Eucharist as Christ's invitation, not a theological barrier.** The Eucharist belongs to Christ, not to us. It is He who invites His people to the table, and it is He who makes us one.

- **Recognize that the world needs to see a united Church.** In an age of deep skepticism and spiritual hunger, the world longs to see a community where love triumphs over division, where grace overcomes pride, and where reconciliation is not just preached but practiced.

The Witness of St. Paul:

The apostle Paul, in his letter to the Ephesians, reminds the Church of the deep spiritual reality that undergirds her unity:

"There is one body and one Spirit, just as also you were called in one hope of your calling; one Lord, one faith, one baptism; one God and Father of all who is over all and through all and in all" (Ephesians 4:4-6).

This is not an ideal to be aspired to in the distant future; it is a present reality to be lived now. The Church is one, whether she acts like it or not. The Eucharistic table, when rightly understood and faithfully practiced, becomes the visible and tangible sign of this oneness — a sign that the world desperately needs to see.

In the following conclusion, we will reflect on the urgent call for reconciliation at the Eucharistic table and the hopeful invitation Christ extends to His divided Church: to become truly one that the world may believe.

Conclusion: A Call to Reconciliation at the Eucharistic Table**

As we come to the close of this chapter, we are left standing before a profound challenge — one that touches the very heart of the Church's identity and mission. The tragedy of Eucharistic separation is not simply a matter of differing opinions, theological disagreements, or ecclesial traditions; it is, at its core, a wound in the Body of Christ.

Throughout this chapter, we have seen that the Eucharist is not a private spiritual exercise or a ritual confined within the walls of any single denomination. It is the living mystery of Christ's self-giving love, the sacrament of unity, and the visible expression of the one Church gathered by the Spirit and called to share in the divine life of God. To stand divided at the Eucharistic table is not just to divide from one another; it is to obscure the very face of Christ to the world.

The Urgency of the Hour:

We live in a time when the world is increasingly fragmented, skeptical, and wounded. People hunger for meaning, for belonging, for truth—and they look, often cautiously, to the Church to see whether the message of Jesus offers something real, something different, something transformative.

What they see, too often, is a Church divided. They see believers who profess love but refuse to reconcile; they see churches that proclaim one Christ but celebrate separate Eucharists; they see a gospel of unity preached from divided altars.

At this moment, the urgency could not be clearer: **the Church must reclaim the Eucharist as the path to unity, not the prize for achieving it.**

What Needs to Change:

To restore Eucharistic unity, we must undergo a profound shift in perspective and practice:

- We must **recover the humility** to acknowledge that unity is a gift of grace, not an achievement of human effort.

- We must **embrace the Eucharist as Christ's invitation**, open to all whom He calls, not a fortress guarded by human gatekeepers.

- We must **prioritize love and reconciliation over rigid legalism**, trusting that in the act of coming together at the Lord's table, the Holy Spirit will do the work of healing, teaching, and drawing us deeper into truth.

This does not mean abandoning the importance of doctrine, nor does it mean ignoring the real differences that exist among Christian traditions. But it does mean recognizing that the Eucharist itself is meant to be a place of encounter, a place where the Church's divisions can be brought into the presence of Christ for healing.

Christ's Invitation to His Church:

The table of the Lord is not ours to divide; it is Christ's to offer. And Christ offers it freely. As He broke bread with His disciples on the night He was betrayed, as He revealed Himself to the disciples at Emmaus, and as He continues to give Himself in the Eucharist today, Jesus extends an invitation to His entire Church:

"Take, eat; this is My body. Drink from it, all of you; for this is My blood of the covenant." (Matthew 26:26-28)

This invitation echoes across time and across every division. It is not the voice of one denomination speaking to another; it is the voice of the Savior calling all His people to the table of grace.

Will We Answer the Call?

The question before us is simple yet searching: **Will we answer Christ's call to be one? Will we dare to trust that in coming together at His table, He will heal our wounds, reconcile our differences, and make us one Body in Him?**

The world is watching. The world is waiting. And the world needs to see a Church that lives the unity it proclaims — a Church that gathers as one family at the one table of the Lord, bearing witness to the reconciling love of God in Christ.

May we, with humility and hope, rise to meet this call — not by our strength, but by the power of the One who prayed, **"That they may all be one... so that the world may believe that You sent Me"** (John 17:21).

Chapter 7

Eucharistic Unity: A Biblical Mandate

The Church today finds itself surrounded by countless divisions—doctrinal splits, denominational walls, and historic grievances that have fractured the visible unity of Christ's people. Yet at the very heart of the Gospel lies a truth that resists such fragmentation: **the Eucharist is God's gift not only of grace but of unity**.

The Eucharist is not merely a sacred rite, a denominational badge, or a theological point for debate. It is the **very center of Christian life**, the **sacrament of Christ's Body and Blood,** by which we are drawn into communion with Him and, through Him, into communion with one another. From the very beginning, God's saving plan has aimed not merely at rescuing isolated individuals but at **gathering people for Himself**—one family, one body, one Church (John 11:52; Ephesians 4:4-6).

We must grasp this truth clearly:

The Eucharist is not only the **result of unity** among Christians, as if we could first achieve perfect agreement and then sit together at Christ's table. Rather, the Eucharist is the **means by which God shapes, heals, and builds that unity**. It is in the Eucharist that we become what we are called to be: **one body in Christ** (1 Corinthians 10:16-17).

This chapter invites us to **reconsider our divisions** in light of the Eucharist. It challenges us to recognize that **unity is not optional**—it is a biblical mandate grounded in the saving work of Christ and expressed most powerfully at His table.

We will walk through four key biblical pillars that illuminate this truth:

1- **Lord Jesus' High Priestly Prayer** (John 17:20-23), where Christ reveals that unity is His passionate desire for His followers.

2- **Christ's Sacrificial Death** (John 11:52), which gathers into one the scattered children of God.

3- **The Eucharist as a Means of Unity** (Ephesians 4:13), not merely a prize for those who already agree.

4- **The Meaning of "Discerning the Body of Christ"** (1 Corinthians 11:29) calls believers to recognize both Christ's real presence and the unity of His Church.

As we explore these biblical truths, we will listen carefully to the witness of the early Church Fathers, who remind us that the Eucharist has always been the **foundation of Christian unity**. Their voices echo the same challenge we face today: **Will we allow the table of Christ to remain a sign of division, or will we embrace it as the place where God's people are reconciled and made one?**

This chapter is not merely a theological reflection—it is a call to action.

The world is watching. As Lord Jesus prayed, "That they may all be one... so that the world may believe that You sent Me" (John 17:21), we must recognize that the Church's unity is a living testimony to the truth of the Gospel. Without Eucharistic unity, we betray that testimony.

Let us approach this chapter humbly, prayerfully, and with the deep conviction that **Christ Himself longs to gather His Church together at His table**. The Eucharist is not only our nourishment for the journey but the **healing of our wounds, the restoration of our divisions, and the manifestation of the one Body of Christ** in the world today.

1. Lord Jesus' High Priestly Prayer: "That They May All Be One" (John 17:20-23)

On the night before His Passion, Lord Jesus lifted His eyes to heaven and offered the most profound and intimate prayer recorded in Scripture—the **High Priestly Prayer** of John 17. This is not merely a prayer for comfort or strength before suffering; it is a **window into the very heart of Christ**, revealing His **deepest longing** for His people.

> "I do not ask on behalf of these alone, but for those also who believe in Me through their word; 21 that they may all be one; even as You, Father, are in Me and I in You, that they also may be in Us, so that the world may believe that You sent Me" (John 17:20-21).

Here, the Lord Jesus prays not only for His disciples who were with Him in the Upper Room but also for **all who would believe in Him through their message**—that is, the entire Church throughout time. His petition centers on a single, burning desire: **that they may all be one**.

Two Central Truths in Jesus' Prayer:

This prayer communicates two essential truths:

- **Unity among believers is meant to reflect the unity of the Father and the Son.** The oneness Jesus desires is not a superficial or merely organizational unity but a deep, spiritual unity that mirrors the **divine communion** between the Father and the Son. This is a unity rooted in love, truth, and shared divine life.

- **This unity is essential for the world to believe in Christ's divine mission.** Jesus ties the credibility of the Gospel to the unity of His followers. He prays "so that the world may believe that You sent Me." Christian unity, then, is not merely an internal concern; it is **missional**. A divided Church weakens its witness before the world, while a united Church becomes a radiant sign of God's reconciling love.

The Eucharist: The Sacrament of Oneness:

How does this unity come about? The answer lies at the heart of Christian worship—the **Eucharist**.

> "Is not the cup of blessing which we bless a sharing in the blood of Christ? Is not the bread which we break a sharing in the body of Christ? Since there is one bread, we who are many are one body, for we all partake of the one bread" (1 Corinthians 10:16-17).

St. Paul teaches that the Eucharist is not merely a symbol of unity but the very **means by which unity is accomplished**. When we partake of the one bread and the one cup, we are not just remembering Christ—we are being **knit together as one body** in Him.

To divide the Eucharistic table, therefore, is to **contradict the very purpose of Christ's gift**. When Christians break communion with one another, whether through historical schisms, doctrinal disputes, or mutual exclusions, they **fracture the unity** that Christ prayed for on the night of His Passion.

The Witness of the Church Fathers:

The early Church understood this connection deeply. **St. Cyril of Alexandria**, in his *Commentary on the Gospel of John*, writes:

> "Christ gave us the sacrament of His Body, not to divide us, but to bind us together in one Spirit."

For St. Cyril, the Eucharist is the Spirit-filled bond of peace. It is not meant to be a **boundary marker** separating Christians but a **healing sacrament** that draws all believers into the life of God.

The Scandal of Disunity at the Table:

When we refuse Eucharistic unity, we do more than fail to honor one another — we **wound Christ Himself**. He has given His Body and Blood precisely so that His people might be made one. The Apostle Paul warns the Corinthians that divisions at the Eucharistic meal nullify its true meaning (1 Corinthians 11:17–22). To approach the table while refusing unity is to **profane the very gift** that Christ offers.

This is why Eucharistic unity is not a **secondary issue**. It strikes at the very heart of the Gospel, at the very heart of Christ's mission.

A Mandate, Not a Suggestion:

If the Lord Jesus prayed for oneness, then unity is not optional—it is a **mandate**. And the Eucharist, far from being a prize reserved for the already-unified, is the very **means by which God builds unity among His people**.

We must reject the idea that the Eucharist can be weaponized as a tool of exclusion. Rather, we must recover the Church's ancient understanding that the Eucharist is **the sacrament of love**, the meal where reconciliation is made possible, and the place where the many become one.

> "There is one body and one Spirit, just as you also were called in one hope of your calling" (Ephesians 4:4).

A Call to Respond:

As we reflect on Christ's High Priestly Prayer, we are faced with a challenge:

- Are we willing to be part of the answer to Jesus' prayer for unity?

- Will we allow the Eucharist to become the place where healing begins?

- Or will we continue to let human divisions block the power of the sacrament that was given to make us one?

The path of Eucharistic unity calls for humility, repentance, and the willingness to **lay down pride and self-interest** for the sake of Christ's Body, the Church. This is no easy path—but it is the one marked out by the pierced hands of the Savior who prayed, suffered, and died to make His people one.

Let us, then, take seriously the call of John 17—not merely as an abstract ideal but as a living, an urgent invitation to embody the unity Christ desires, beginning at **His table**.

2. "He Died to Gather Into One the Scattered Children of God" (John 11:52)

As the Gospel of John draws us into the events leading up to the Passion, we encounter a striking and often overlooked declaration about the purpose of Jesus' death:

"Now he [Caiaphas] did not say this from himself, but being high priest that year, he prophesied that Jesus was going to die for the nation, and not for the nation only, but in order that He might also gather together into one the children of God who are scattered abroad" (John 11:51-52).

Even in the mouth of an unwitting high priest, the Spirit reveals God's redemptive plan: **the death of Jesus was not simply to save individuals in isolation** but to gather the scattered people of God into **one united family**.

Christ's Death: More Than Individual Salvation

Too often, modern Christianity has reduced the meaning of the cross to a purely personal transaction: **Jesus died for my sins to give me forgiveness and eternal life**. While this is gloriously true, the Gospel speaks of something even larger.

The purpose of Christ's death, according to John, is both **for the nation** (the people of Israel) and for the scattered children of God across the world—**to gather them into one**. The cross is the ultimate act of divine reconciliation, breaking down the dividing walls between peoples (Ephesians 2:14-16) and **forming one new humanity** in Christ.

This means that when we come to the Eucharist, we do not come as isolated individuals seeking private spiritual blessings. We come as members of the one Body, reconciled not only to God but to one another through the blood of Christ.

> "For He Himself is our peace, who made both groups one and broke down the dividing wall of the partition by abolishing in His flesh the enmity, the Law of commandments contained in ordinances, so that in Himself He might create the two into one new man, making peace" (Ephesians 2:14-15).

The Eucharist: The Sacrament of Gathered Unity

The Eucharist is the sacrament that enacts and embodies this gathered unity. In the breaking of the bread, the many become one. In the sharing of the cup, the scattered are drawn together into the life of Christ.

> "Since there is one bread, we who are many are one body, for we all partake of the one bread" (1 Corinthians 10:17).

This truth is not just a beautiful theological idea—it is a **challenge** to the Church today. How can we claim to share in the one Bread while remaining divided at the table of the Lord? How can we profess that Christ died to unite us and yet allow old wounds, theological quarrels, or cultural differences to keep us apart in the very place where His Body and Blood are offered?

The Witness of the Early Church:

The early Church understood the Eucharist as the fulfillment of Christ's gathering work. **St. Irenaeus of Lyons** (2nd century), reflecting on the Eucharist, draws a powerful image from the natural world:

> "Just as the scattered grains of wheat are gathered to form one bread, so too are we gathered into the one Body of Christ through the Eucharist" (Against Heresies 4.18.5).

This image is striking. The Eucharist takes what are many and scattered—grains, grapes, people, nations—and gathers them into one new reality: the Body of Christ. For Irenaeus, the Eucharist is not simply a symbol of unity; it is the very act by which God draws His people into unity with Himself and with one another.

Division at the Table: A Betrayal of the Cross

To remain divided at the Eucharistic table is to **contradict the purpose of Christ's sacrifice**. It is to deny the reconciling power of His death and to resist the Spirit who gathers the scattered into one.

> "Who Himself bore our sins in His body on the tree, so that having died to sin, we might live to righteousness; by His wounds you were healed. For you were continually straying like sheep, but now you have returned to the Shepherd and Overseer of your souls" (1 Peter 2:24-25).

The Eucharist is the celebration of this healing, this return, this reconciliation. Yet how can we claim to be healed if we still live in division? How can we claim to be gathered if we continue to scatter ourselves?

A Call to Eucharistic Repentance:

If Christ died to gather the scattered children of God, then we who gather at His table must examine our hearts and our communities. We are called to repent of the divisions we have inherited or sustained. We are called to seek the unity that Christ purchased at the price of His blood.

This is not merely an ecumenical project or a denominational aspiration. It is a **Gospel imperative** — a call to live out what Christ has already accomplished.

> "Therefore, accept one another, just as Christ also accepted us to the glory of God" (Romans 15:7).

Reflection:

If Christ **died to unite us**, how can we justify remaining divided at His table?

- What old grievances, traditions, or misunderstandings stand in the way of Eucharistic unity today?
- Are we willing to let the cross reshape our relationships, our worship, and our identity as the gathered people of God?

As we move deeper into this chapter, let us carry with us the sobering and hopeful truth that the Eucharist is not just a ritual but the living sign of the unity Christ died to create. To share in the Eucharist is to proclaim, by word and deed, that we are one body, reconciled and gathered in Him.

3. The Eucharist as the Means, Not Just the Result, of Unity (Ephesians 4:13)

In many Christian circles today, there is an assumption that **unity must come first** before believers can approach the Eucharistic table together. The reasoning often goes like this: once we resolve our doctrinal disagreements, heal our historic wounds, and arrive at a full agreement, only then can we share in the sacred meal of the Body and Blood of Christ. But Scripture offers us a different—and profoundly more hopeful—vision.

"Until we all attain to the unity of the faith, and of the full knowledge of the Son of God, to a mature man, to the measure of the stature which belongs to the fullness of Christ" (Ephesians 4:13).

In this passage, St. Paul is clear: **the unity of the faith** is not something we possess perfectly today; it is something we are **growing toward**. It is a goal, not a prerequisite. And the Eucharist, far from being the reward we receive once we reach that goal, is actually **the means by which we journey toward it**.

Why the Eucharist Is a Means of Unity:

The Eucharist is not merely a ritual reflecting an already-achieved unity of faith. It is the very act through which Christ draws His people into deeper communion with Himself and one another.

When believers gather at the Eucharistic table, they come not as those who have mastered perfect agreement or flawless theology but as those who hunger and thirst for the life of

Christ. In receiving the one Bread and one Cup, they are being **formed** into the one Body of Christ.

"For also by one Spirit we were all baptized into one body, whether Jews or Greeks, whether slaves or free, and we were all made to drink of one Spirit" (1 Corinthians 12:13).

This divine shaping is ongoing. It is through **sharing in Christ's Body** that we come to understand, experience, and live out our unity in Him. True Christian unity **flows from the Eucharist**, not the other way around.

This truth calls us to humility. It reminds us that unity is not something we can manufacture by human effort alone. It is a gift given by God, nurtured at His table, and sustained by His Spirit.

The Witness of the Early Church:

The earliest Christians understood this deeply. The book of Acts tells us that the first believers **devoted themselves to the apostles' teaching, fellowship, the breaking of bread, and prayer** (Acts 2:42). These were not separate activities; they were woven together into one life of communal worship, discipleship, and Eucharistic fellowship.

Crucially, the early Christians did not wait for complete doctrinal alignment before breaking bread together. They knew that it was precisely in **Eucharistic participation** that they were shaped into one body.

St. John Chrysostom, preaching in the fourth century, offered this sharp and pastoral warning:

> "Would you honor the Body of Christ? Then do not exclude your brother from the Eucharistic table. For if you break this unity, you have wounded Christ Himself" (Homily on Matthew 50.3).

For Chrysostom, honoring the Eucharist meant more than venerating the sacramental elements; it meant **embracing one's fellow believers** as co-members of Christ's Body. To exclude a brother or sister from the table was not merely a social error—it was a spiritual wound inflicted on Christ Himself.

Unity as a Process, Not a Prerequisite

One of the greatest misunderstandings in the modern Church is the belief that Eucharistic communion must wait until we have achieved **complete theological harmony**. But if this were true, the Church would never celebrate the Eucharist at all. Throughout Christian history, believers have lived with real differences in understanding, yet they have continued to gather at the Lord's table because they understood that **it is there, at the table, that Christ Himself draws us toward unity**.

This is why we must see the Eucharist as a **divine instrument of reconciliation**. It does not erase differences overnight, but it opens the way for love, humility, and shared life to take root and grow.

> "Being diligent in keeping the unity of the Spirit in the bond of peace. There is one body and one Spirit, just as also you were called in one hope of your calling" (Ephesians 4:3–4).

A Call to Eucharistic Openness:

Rather than demanding **perfection before communion**, we are called to recognize the Eucharist as the place where Christ works to bring us to maturity. It is at the altar that our pride is humbled, our divisions are softened, and our common identity in Christ is renewed.

This does not mean that serious doctrinal differences are unimportant. But it does mean that Eucharistic exclusion, when wielded carelessly or pridefully, can actually hinder the very work of unity that Christ desires.

Reflection:

- Are we approaching the Eucharist as a **means of unity** or merely as a reward for already achieved theological agreement?

- How might our Eucharistic practice change if we truly believed that it is Christ Himself who shapes our unity at His table?

- Are we willing to open our hearts, and perhaps even our altars, to the reconciling work of God?

As we reflect on this section, let us remember that **the Eucharist is not our achievement**. It is the gift of Christ, given to make us one. The road to unity is long, but it begins — and is sustained — at the table where the broken Bread of Life is offered for the life of the world.

4. What It Means to "Discern the Body of Christ" (1 Corinthians 11:29)

Few passages in Scripture have caused as much confusion and debate over Eucharistic practice as **St. Paul's warning to the Corinthians** about the dangers of approaching the Lord's Table in an unworthy manner.

> "For he who eats and drinks, eats and drinks judgment to himself if he does not judge [Discern] the body rightly" (1 Corinthians 11:29).

At first glance, many readers assume this warning is about **doctrinal correctness**—that only those with fully aligned beliefs may partake—or that it is about moral perfection, barring sinners from the table. But to read the passage this way is to miss the profound and challenging context of Paul's words.

The Context of St. Paul's Rebuke:

St. Paul was not addressing abstract theological disputes. He was confronting a **specific abuse** happening within the Corinthian church.

> "For, in the first place, when you come together as a church, I hear that divisions exist among you, and in part, I believe it. For in your eating, each one takes his own supper first, and one is hungry and another is drunk. Do you not have houses in which to eat and drink? Or do you despise the church of God and shame those who have nothing? What shall I say to you? Shall I praise you? In this, I will not praise you" (1 Corinthians 11:18, 21–22).

The Corinthian Christians were turning the Eucharistic gathering into a **social event marked by inequality and exclusion**. The wealthy feasted, while the poor went hungry. They were failing to recognize that the Lord's Supper was meant to express the **unity and mutual love** of the Body of Christ—not to reinforce social divisions.

To Discern the Body: Two-Fold Meaning

St. Paul's command to "discern the body" carries a **double meaning**:

1- **Recognizing Christ's real presence in the Eucharist.** The bread and the wine are not ordinary food and drink; they are the Body and Blood of the Lord. To approach the table carelessly, as though it were just another meal, is to fail to honor the sacred mystery.

2- **Recognizing the gathered Church as the Body of Christ.** St. Paul uses the phrase "Body of Christ" not only for the sacrament but also for the community of believers (1 Corinthians 12:27). To fail to care for one's fellow believers—to allow divisions, resentment, or neglect—while partaking of the sacrament is to **contradict the meaning** of the Eucharist itself.

> "Since there is one bread, we who are many are one body, for we all partake of the one bread" (1 Corinthians 10:17).

To discern the Body, then, is not merely about personal piety but about **communal responsibility**. It is a call to examine how we live as a community united in Christ, reflecting His love and holiness.

Exclusion from the Eucharist vs. Exclusion of Others

A critical point often missed is that St. Paul does **not** suggest that some should be barred from receiving the Eucharist based on doctrinal disagreements or personal unworthiness. Rather, he warns that **division itself** — whether social, economic, or spiritual — is what makes one unworthy.

It is not that we should withhold the Eucharist from others but that we should not come to the table while **harboring division in our hearts** or ignoring the needs of our brothers and sisters.

St. Augustine, in his *Sermon 272*, puts it sharply:

> "To receive the Eucharist without seeking unity is to drink judgment upon oneself. The Table of the Lord is meant for peace, not division."

In other words, the Eucharist is not a prize for the righteous or a weapon for the doctrinally pure. It is a sacrament of reconciliation, a place where sinners are healed, and the divided are made one. Withholding the Eucharist because of division **only deepens the very sin St. Paul warns against**.

A Radical Challenge:

St. Paul's teaching confronts us with a radical challenge. The question is not, "Who is pure enough to approach the table?" but rather, "Are we as a community living the unity that the Eucharist proclaims?"

When we come to the Lord's Table, we are proclaiming:

- That we are one Body in Christ.

- That we share one hope, one faith, one baptism.

- That we are reconciled to God and one another.

If we approach the Eucharist without seeking reconciliation—without caring for the unity of the Church—we fail to discern the Body.

Reflection:

- How do we, as individuals and communities, **prepare our hearts** to discern the Body of Christ before approaching the Eucharist?

- Are there divisions, resentments, or exclusions within our churches that we need to confront and heal?

- How can we more fully live out the truth that the Eucharist is the sacrament of unity, peace, and reconciliation?

A Call to Healing:

As we reflect on St. Paul's words, we are invited into a posture of **humble repentance and hope**. The Eucharist is not only a mirror exposing our divisions but a means of healing them. Christ offers Himself as the Bread of Life so that His broken Body might make us whole.

Let us, then, come to His table with reverence, with love for one another, and with a deep commitment to live as one Body united in Him.

Conclusion: The Eucharist is the Key to Church Unity

As we reach the close of this chapter, we are invited to step back and behold the great mystery we have been reflecting on: the Eucharist is not a **prize for perfect theology**, nor a **reward for doctrinal agreement**, but the very **means through which Christ Himself builds His Church into unity**.

From every angle, Scripture and tradition point us toward this truth:

- **Lord Jesus prayed for unity** in His High Priestly Prayer (John 17:21), longing that His followers might be one as He and the Father are one. The Eucharist must be a visible and living reflection of that prayer, not a contradiction of it.

- **Christ died to unite believers** (John 11:52), gathering into one the scattered children of God. His sacrifice on the cross was not only about individual redemption but about forming a reconciled people, a new humanity. The Eucharist is the sign and sacrament of this unity — a unity purchased at the price of His Blood.

- **Unity is the goal, not the prerequisite, for Eucharistic communion** (Ephesians 4:13). St. Paul makes it clear that we are all moving toward the fullness of unity in Christ, but we are not there yet. We are still growing, still being formed, maturing — and the Eucharist is one of God's primary means to bring us there.

- **To discern the Body of Christ** is to seek unity, not division (1 Corinthians 11:29). St. Paul's warning is not about fencing off the Eucharist from the imperfect but about confronting the real dangers of harboring division, neglecting the poor, and failing to love the members of Christ's Body.

The Eucharist as a Starting Point, Not an End Point

If we truly desire to heal Christian divisions, the Eucharist must be our starting point—not merely our goal. We cannot wait until every difference is resolved or every wound is healed before we come together at Christ's table. Instead, we must **let the Eucharist itself become the place where reconciliation begins**.

When we come to the altar, we do not come with our own perfection. We come empty-handed, hungry, and in need of grace. And there, Christ meets us—not just individually, but corporately, as His people. He gives us His Body so that we might become His Body.

> "There is one body and one Spirit, just as also you were called in one hope of your calling; one Lord, one faith, one baptism; one God and Father of all who is over all and through all and in all" (Ephesians 4:4-6).

A Call to the Church:

The Eucharist stands at the center of the Church's life—not as a mark of division, but as a sign of unity. We are called to embody this unity in our worship, in our relationships, and our mission to the world.

The challenge is clear:

- Will we continue to let the Eucharist divide us, treating it as a badge of separation?

- Or will we let it become the healing sacrament Christ intended, where believers are reconciled to God and one another?

Christ **gave us His Body to unite us**. He invites us to come to His table, not as isolated individuals, but as members of one Body, drawn together by one Spirit and bound together in one hope.

The Path Forward:

The path to Christian unity begins not in councils or committees but **at the altar**—where Christ Himself makes us one. If we are willing to approach the Eucharist with humility, with love for our brothers and sisters, and with a deep desire for reconciliation, we will find that unity is not beyond our reach. It is already being offered to us, week by week, at the table of the Lord.

Let us then come to the Eucharist with hearts open to the prayer of Jesus, the sacrifice of the cross, the work of the Spirit, and the unity of the Church. For at the altar, Christ gathers His people into one—and there, the world will see that the Father has indeed sent the Son.

Chapter 8

A Renewed Eucharistic Theology for Unity

The divisions among Christians at the Eucharistic table strike at the very heart of the Gospel message. The Eucharist, instituted by Christ as the **sacrament of His Body and Blood**, was meant to unite His people in communion with Himself and with one another. Yet today, it has too often become a point of separation—a line drawn in the sand between denominations, traditions, and confessions.

We must confront the serious **theological and pastoral questions** these divisions raise. Should the Eucharist be the **goal** of Christian unity or its **prerequisite**? Are we right to insist on **full doctrinal agreement** before welcoming one another to the Lord's table? Can we uphold the mystery of **sacramental realism** — that is, the true presence of Christ in the Eucharist—without slipping into **ecclesial exclusivism**, turning the sacrament into a guarded prize rather than a healing gift?

These questions are not merely theoretical. They touch the deepest longings of Christ's Church and the urgent needs of a divided world.

A Path Backward to Move Forward;

This chapter proposes that a path forward may be found by **returning to the early Church's vision** of the Eucharist—a vision grounded in Scripture, nourished by the Church Fathers, and lived out by the first Christian communities. Before theological debates hardened into divisions, before denominational barriers were erected, the Eucharist was understood as the **beating heart of Christian life**, a source of unity and grace.

By recovering this vision, we may rediscover the theological tools and spiritual posture necessary for the renewal of **Eucharistic unity** today.

What This Chapter Will Explore:

In the sections that follow, we will explore four essential dimensions:

1- **Unity in the Eucharist: A Return to the Early Church's Vision**

   We will look at how the first Christians saw the Eucharist not as a reward for unity already achieved but as the **foundation upon which unity was built**.

2- **Is Full Doctrinal Agreement Necessary Before Eucharistic Sharing?**

   We will wrestle with the common assumption that theological consensus must precede Eucharistic communion, and we will examine what Scripture and tradition suggest about this relationship.

3- **Sacramental Realism vs. Ecclesial Exclusivism: Can We Embrace Both?**

   We will explore how the Church can affirm the sacred mystery of Christ's real presence in the Eucharist without turning the sacrament into a barrier that deepens division.

4- **The Church as a Hospital for Sinners, Not a Reward for the Righteous**

We will reflect on the Eucharist's role as a **means of healing, grace, and transformation**, not merely as a privilege reserved for the theologically or morally perfect.

The Hope of Renewal

By rediscovering the **depth, beauty, and purpose** of the Eucharist, we may find the key to restoring Christian unity — not just as an abstract ideal but as a lived and visible reality at the Lord's table. The Eucharist, after all, is not ours to control or to guard jealously. It is Christ's gift to His Church, given so that His scattered children may be gathered into one Body, sharing one Bread, drinking one Cup, and living in one Spirit.

As we journey through this chapter, let us do so with **humble hearts** — open to the possibility that the divisions we have long assumed to be permanent might, in fact, be healed by the very sacrament we have too often used to reinforce them.

Let us return to the altar, where Christ Himself waits to make us one.

1. Unity in the Eucharist: A Return to the Early Church's Vision

To recover a renewed Eucharistic theology for Christian unity, we must first look back — not nostalgically, but faithfully—at how the early Church understood and lived out the Eucharist. For the earliest Christians, the Eucharist was not an isolated ritual, nor was it a reward reserved for the theologically advanced. It was the **center of Christian life**, the **beating heart** of the community, and the **bond of unity** that drew together believers from every walk of life.

The Early Church's Eucharistic Fellowship:

The book of Acts gives us one of the clearest pictures of the Church's earliest life together:

"And they were continually devoting themselves to the apostles' teaching and to the fellowship, to the breaking of bread and to the prayers" (Acts 2:42).

The "breaking of bread" here refers not merely to ordinary meals but to the Eucharistic celebration—a sacred meal that bound the community together in worship, love, and shared life. This was not a marginal practice; it was a central and defining act of the Church's existence.

St. Paul affirms this in his first letter to the Corinthians:

> "Is not the cup of blessing which we bless a sharing in the blood of Christ? Is not the bread which we break a sharing in the body of Christ? 17 Since there is one bread, we who are many are one body, for we all partake of the one bread" (1 Corinthians 10:16-17).

Here, Paul reveals a profound mystery: the Eucharist not only signifies but **affects** the unity of the Church. In partaking of the one loaf, believers become the one Body of Christ. Unity is not something added later — it is forged and nourished at the Eucharistic table itself.

The **Didache**, one of the earliest Christian writings outside the New Testament (dating from the late first or early second century), captures this same understanding:

> "Even as this broken bread was scattered over the hills, and was gathered together and became one, so let Your Church be gathered together from the ends of the earth into Your kingdom" (Didache 9:4).

In other words, the Eucharist is the moment when the many are gathered into one — not only locally but across space and time, drawing believers from every place into the one kingdom of God.

Eucharistic Unity in the Early Centuries:

The testimony of the early Church Fathers further confirms this vision.

St. Ignatius of Antioch, writing around 107 AD on his way to martyrdom, urged the Christians in Philadelphia:

> "Take care to participate in one Eucharist, for there is one flesh of our Lord Jesus Christ and one cup that leads to unity in His blood; there is one altar, just as there is one bishop along with the presbytery and deacons" (Letter to the Philadelphians 4).

For St. Ignatius, the unity of the Church was visibly and sacramentally expressed in the Eucharist. To break communion at the altar was to **undermine the unity** established by Christ Himself.

A century later, **St. Cyprian of Carthage** would echo the same conviction:

> "God is one, and Christ is one, and His Church is one; one faith and one people joined together in the bond of unity" (On the Unity of the Church 6).

For Cyprian, the unity of the Church was not an optional ideal but a **sacramental reality** rooted in the one Body and Blood of Christ. The Eucharist was both the sign and the instrument of this unity, making the Church visibly one across time, space, and culture.

A Vision Lost?

Yet today, divisions at the Eucharistic table are widespread and often fiercely defended. Denominational barriers, theological disputes, historical wounds, and cultural separations have turned the Eucharist—intended by Christ as the **supreme sign of unity**—into a point of exclusion and division.

We must honestly ask: **Has the Church placed barriers where Christ intended a bridge?**

- Have we allowed human boundaries to overshadow divine grace?

- Have we turned the Eucharist into a badge of identity rather than a sacrament of reconciliation?

- Have we forgotten that the early Church saw the Eucharist not as the prize for unity achieved but as the foundation upon which unity was built?

A Call to Recover the Early Vision:

Suppose we hope to move toward renewed Eucharistic unity. In that case, we must reclaim the early Church's understanding of the Eucharist as the center of Christian life and the source of communion among believers. This will require humility, repentance, and a fresh attentiveness to Scripture and tradition.

The Eucharist is not ours to control. It is Christ's gift to His Church—given not to reinforce division but to heal it. If we would honor the Lord's table, we must return to the altar with open hands, open hearts, and a renewed commitment to live as one Body, gathered and sustained by the Bread of Life.

2. Is Full Doctrinal Agreement Necessary Before Eucharistic Sharing?

One of the most sensitive and debated questions in the life of the Church is this: **Must Christians agree fully on every point of doctrine before they can share the Eucharist together?** Many Christian traditions hold that Eucharistic communion presupposes full theological agreement, particularly regarding doctrines of salvation, the Church, and the nature of the Eucharist itself. But is this understanding supported by Scripture and the witness of the early Church?

This section will explore whether **doctrinal perfection is a necessary precondition for Eucharistic sharing** or whether the Eucharist itself can be a means by which Christ draws His people into deeper unity and truth.

Biblical Insights on Unity Before Doctrine:

The New Testament offers several striking examples where fellowship around Christ preceded complete theological understanding.

The Lord Jesus Shared Meals with Sinners and Outcasts

> "And Levi gave a big reception for Him in his house, and there was a great crowd of tax collectors and other people who were reclining at the table with them. And the Pharisees and their scribes began grumbling at His disciples, saying, "Why do you eat and drink with the tax collectors and sinners?" And Jesus answered and said to them, "It is not those who are well who need a physician, but those who are sick" (Luke 5:29-31).

Jesus' practice of sharing meals — signs of communion and welcome — with those on the margins shows that He did not wait for perfect repentance or doctrinal understanding before extending His table. Rather, it was through His fellowship that many came to know and follow Him.

The Disciples on the Road to Emmaus:

> "And it happened that when He had reclined at the table with them, He took the bread and blessed it, and after breaking it, He was giving it to them. 31 Then their eyes were opened, and they recognized Him. And He vanished from their sight" (Luke 24:30-31).

The two disciples did not recognize the risen Lord until **He broke bread with them**. Their understanding came not first through theological explanation but through the Eucharistic act itself.

The First Christians Grew Together in Understanding

"And they were continually devoting themselves to the apostles' teaching and to the fellowship, to the breaking of bread and to the prayers" (Acts 2:42).

The early Church did not wait for a complete consensus on all matters of faith before gathering around the Eucharist. Instead, they **grew together** through shared worship, teaching, and sacramental life.

The Witness of the Church Fathers:

St. John Chrysostom offers profound wisdom on this point:

> "It is not right to require perfect understanding before receiving the Eucharist. For it is in the Eucharist that Christ is revealed, as He was to the disciples at Emmaus" (Homily on Luke 24).

St. Chrysostom's insight challenges the idea that the Eucharist is reserved for the doctrinally advanced. Rather, it is in the breaking of the bread that Christ reveals Himself and draws His people deeper into communion with Him and with one another.

A Call for a Renewed Perspective:

Rather than demanding **theological perfection** before communion, a renewed Eucharistic theology invites us to see the Eucharist as a **means by which believers are drawn into deeper truth and unity**.

If the Eucharist is truly Christ Himself, can we rightly refuse to share Christ with those who sincerely seek Him, even if they have not yet arrived at full doctrinal agreement?

St. Augustine speaks directly to this tension:

> "Recognize in the bread what hung on the Cross, and in the cup what flowed from His side. If you receive it, you must also be one in heart and spirit with those who share it" (Sermon 272).

For Augustine, receiving the Eucharist is not merely an act of personal devotion but a communal commitment. It binds believers together, even in their differences, because it is Christ who is shared.

Unity as a Journey:

Christian unity is not a static achievement — it is a **journey**. The Eucharist is not only the sign of unity already reached but the very **pathway along which unity grows**.

This does not mean ignoring theological differences or diminishing the importance of truth. It means recognizing that the Eucharist, as the sacrament of Christ's presence, can be a powerful instrument of reconciliation, healing, and illumination.

Reflection:

- Are we using doctrinal disagreements as **barriers to communion** rather than invitations to deeper dialogue and shared life?

- How might a renewed understanding of the Eucharist as **both the source and the goal of unity** reshape the Church's pastoral and ecumenical practices today?

- Are we willing to trust that Christ Himself, present in the Eucharist, can draw His people together—even across the boundaries we have inherited or built?

As we continue through this chapter, let us remember that **the Eucharist belongs to Christ**. It is He who invites, He who nourishes, and He who makes His people one.

3. Sacramental Realism vs. Ecclesial Exclusivism: Can We Embrace Both?

Throughout the centuries, the Church has wrestled with a profound tension: how to uphold the **sacred mystery of the Eucharist** while avoiding the temptation to turn it into a **tool of exclusion**. On one hand, many Christian traditions affirm **sacramental realism**—the belief that the Eucharist is truly the Body and Blood of Christ, not merely symbolic or metaphorical. On the other hand, in the effort to safeguard this sacred reality, the Church has often practiced **ecclesial exclusivism**, restricting Eucharistic participation only to members within its own fold, sometimes even within narrow doctrinal or denominational boundaries.

This raises the central question: Is it possible to uphold both the sanctity of the Eucharist and a more inclusive vision of the Church's unity? Can we affirm sacramental realism without falling into sacramental exclusivism?

Sacramental Realism: The Eucharist as Christ's True Body and Blood

The testimony of Scripture is clear: the Eucharist is no mere memorial. It is the real and life-giving presence of Christ.

"Truly, truly, I say to you, unless you eat the flesh of the Son of Man and drink His blood, you have no life in yourselves" (John 6:53).

St. Paul affirms this sacred reality and warns against receiving the Eucharist **unworthily**:

"Therefore, whoever eats the bread or drinks the cup of the Lord in an unworthy manner shall be guilty of the body and the blood of the Lord" (1 Corinthians 11:27).

Throughout history, the Church has rightly guarded the Eucharist with reverence and care. Sacramental realism insists that the Eucharist is not a human invention but a divine gift and that to approach it casually or profanely is to dishonor the Body and Blood of Christ.

Ecclesial Exclusivism: A Barrier to Christian Unity?

Yet here, we encounter a challenge. In the zeal to protect the holiness of the Eucharist, the Church has often drawn **sharp boundaries** around the table, restricting access to those who meet specific ecclesial or doctrinal criteria.

- Catholic and Orthodox traditions generally practice **closed communion**, inviting only those who are formally in communion with their Church.

- Many Protestant traditions fence the table around particular beliefs about salvation, baptism, or the meaning of the Eucharist.

While these practices aim to safeguard sacramental integrity, they can also **reinforce Christian disunity**. Instead of seeing the Eucharist as a means of drawing believers into deeper unity, it is often treated as the final confirmation of a unity already perfectly established.

But is this the vision of the early Church?

The Witness of the Church Fathers:

St. Irenaeus of Lyons, writing in the second century, reminds us that the Eucharist is not a private possession of any one group:

> "The Eucharist is not a private possession, nor the meal of one sect, but the gift of Christ to His whole Church" (Against Heresies 4.18.5).

For Irenaeus, the Eucharist belongs to Christ — and through Christ, it belongs to the whole Church. It is not the exclusive meal of one faction but the sacrament by which God gathers His people into one Body.

A Possible Way Forward:

Is it possible to hold together a high view of the Eucharist and a more open vision of ecclesial unity? The answer may lie in three essential commitments:

1- **Maintain a high view of the Eucharist as Christ's true Body and Blood.**

   We should never reduce the Eucharist to a mere symbol or deny its transformative power. The Eucharist is holy, and it should be approached with reverence, preparation, and faith.

2- **Avoid using the Eucharist as a weapon of exclusion.**

   We must resist the temptation to turn the Eucharist into a boundary marker that separates "insiders" from "outsiders." While pastoral safeguards are necessary, we must remember that the Eucharist was given as a gift to **heal divisions**, not to deepen them.

3- **Foster dialogue and mutual understanding across traditions.**

   Eucharistic inclusivity does not mean abandoning truth or collapsing all differences. It means engaging in honest, prayerful dialogue, recognizing the presence of Christ in one another, and allowing the Eucharist itself to deepen our shared life in Him.

The Eucharist as Christ's Gift:

If Christ is truly present in the Eucharist, we must ask: **Whose Eucharist is it?**

- Is it the possession of one tradition, one denomination, or one theological framework?

- Or is it the gift of the crucified and risen Lord, given to gather all His people into one?

We must remember: It is Christ who gives Himself in the Eucharist—not the Church, not the priest, not the theologian. It is Christ who invites, who nourishes, and who heals.

Reflection:

1- How can we, as the Church, maintain the holiness of the Eucharist while also embracing its call to unity?

2- Are there practices in our communities that **protect the sacrament** but unintentionally **exclude those whom Christ may be calling**?

3- How can we cultivate a Eucharistic vision that is both theologically faithful and pastorally generous?

As we move forward, let us pray for the grace to hold together the mystery of Christ's real presence with the expansive generosity of His love. For at the altar, we encounter not only the Lord who is holy but the Lord who is **for us all**.

4. The Church as a Hospital for Sinners, Not a Reward for the Righteous

One of the most profound distortions in the Church's understanding of the Eucharist is the belief that it is primarily **a reward for the morally or doctrinally perfected**. This view — though often unspoken—lurks beneath many practices of

Eucharistic exclusion, fencing the table in such a way that only the "worthy," the "pure," or the "correct" are admitted. But is this how Christ intended His table to function?

From the witness of Scripture, the teaching of the early Church, and the best of Christian tradition, we find a very different vision: **the Church is not a club for the spiritually elite; it is a hospital for sinners**. And the Eucharist is not the trophy case of the righteous but the healing medicine offered by Christ Himself.

The Biblical View: The Eucharist as Healing and Nourishment

Throughout the Gospels, we see Jesus reaching out not to the religiously perfect but to the broken, the marginalized, and the sinful.

> "And the Pharisees and their scribes began grumbling at His disciples, saying, "Why do you eat and drink with the tax collectors and sinners?" And Jesus answered and said to them, "It is not those who are well who need a physician, but those who are sick. I have not come to call the righteous but sinners to repentance" (Luke 5:30–32).

Jesus' table was always marked by **mercy and invitation**, not by exclusivity. And this same pattern shapes the Eucharistic meal. The Bread of Life is given not to those who have achieved perfection but to those who hunger and thirst for God.

St. Paul emphasizes this when he writes:

> "But a man must test [examine] himself, and in so doing he is to eat of the bread and drink of the cup" (1 Corinthians 11:28).

Notice: Paul does not say, "Let the community exclude the imperfect," but "Let each one examine themselves" — an invitation to humble self-reflection, not corporate exclusion.

The Witness of the Early Church:

St. Cyril of Jerusalem beautifully captures the healing nature of the Eucharist in his catechetical writings:

> "Do not say, 'I am unworthy.' Instead, draw near in faith, for the Eucharist is not given to the perfect, but to those who seek healing" (*Mystagogical Catechesis* 5).

Cyril's words remind us that no one comes to the Eucharist on their own merits. We all come as beggars, as sinners in need of grace, as souls in need of the medicine of immortality.

The Church as a Hospital:

The early Church often described itself as a **hospital** rather than a courtroom or a social club. This image has deep theological significance:

- In a courtroom, the guilty are excluded.

- In a social club, only the qualified are admitted.

- But in a hospital, the sick are welcomed, the wounded are treated, and the suffering are made whole.

The Eucharist, then, is the sacramental center of this healing ministry. It is Christ's own Body and Blood given to restore, cleanse, and strengthen His people.

When we treat the Eucharist as a reward only for the righteous, we miss its true purpose and rob it of its transformative power.

A Call to Open the Eucharistic Table:

This does not mean ignoring preparation, repentance, or reverence. The Church must always call people to come to the Eucharist with humility, with confession, and with an open heart. But it does mean rejecting the idea that only the flawless are welcome.

- If the Eucharist is a **means of grace**, then restricting it too narrowly hinders the very work Christ intends to do.

- If the Eucharist is a **source of transformation**, then we must invite people to receive Christ so that they may be healed and renewed.

- If the Church is truly the **Body of Christ**, it must be marked by the same mercy, welcome, and love that the Lord Jesus Himself displayed in His earthly ministry.

Reflection:

- Do we approach the Eucharist as **spiritually hungry people seeking Christ's nourishment** or as those who believe we have earned the right to come?

- Are our communities welcoming those who need healing, or are we unintentionally creating barriers that keep people away from the very grace they need?

- How can we better embody the vision of the Church as a **hospital for sinners**, where the Eucharist is offered as Christ's healing gift to all who seek Him?

A Final Challenge:

The Eucharist is where Christ meets His people—not as judge or gatekeeper, but as Savior and healer. Let us open our hearts and our tables to the breadth of His mercy. For in doing so, we not only honor the sacrament itself but participate in the reconciling work of God, drawing His scattered children into one Body, healed and made whole by His love.

Conclusion: The Eucharist as the Key to Christian Unity

As we reach the close of this chapter, we return to the central conviction that has guided our exploration: the Eucharist is not a theological accessory or an optional ritual in the life of the Church. It is the very **heart** of Christian unity, the place where Christ gathers His people into one Body, nourishes them with His own life and sends them forth as witnesses to the world.

To renew our Eucharistic theology for the sake of Christian unity, we must reclaim four essential truths:

1- **The Eucharist must return to its role as the source of unity, not merely its result.**

The early Church did not wait for perfect agreement before gathering around the Lord's table. Rather, it was through the shared breaking of bread that believers were formed and sustained as one Body (Acts 2:42; 1 Corinthians 10:16–17).

2- **Doctrinal unity should be a goal, not a precondition, for Eucharistic sharing.**

While truth matters deeply, the journey toward full understanding is one we undertake together, nourished by the grace of the Eucharist. As the disciples on the road to Emmaus discovered, Christ often reveals Himself most powerfully in the breaking of the bread (Luke 24:30–31).

3- **We can affirm Christ's real presence in the Eucharist while embracing Eucharistic inclusivity.**

Sacramental realism and ecclesial generosity are not opposites. To truly honor Christ's presence in the Eucharist is to recognize that He gives Himself for the healing and unity of His whole Church—not to entrench divisions, but to overcome them (John 6:53–56; Ephesians 4:4–6).

4- **The Church must see the Eucharist as a hospital for sinners, not a reward for theological precision.**

Christ's table is a place of mercy, healing, and transformation. To turn it into a prize for the righteous or a test of intellectual mastery is to betray its true purpose (Luke 5:30–32; 1 Corinthians 11:28; *Evangelii Gaudium*, 47).

The Challenge and the Invitation:

If we truly seek Christian unity, we cannot postpone the conversation about the Eucharist until every doctrinal difference is resolved. Nor can we hide behind the safety of exclusivist practices that protect our theological systems but fracture the Body of Christ.

Instead, we must come to the altar **together** — in humility, repentance, and hope. We must trust that it is Christ who invites us, Christ who feeds us, and Christ who makes us one.

> "There is one body and one Spirit, just as also you were called in one hope of your calling; one Lord, one faith, one baptism; one God and Father of all who is over all and through all and in all" (Ephesians 4:4-6).

A Final Reflection:

The Eucharist is the key to Christian unity because it is Christ Himself who gives it. It is at His table that the walls of division can begin to crumble, where strangers become brothers and sisters, where sinners receive healing, and where the scattered are gathered into one.

Let us, then, open our hands and our hearts to receive the Bread of Life — not as a private possession or a denominational badge, but as the common meal of God's reconciled people. And let us pray that, through this sacrament, the Church may once again shine as a living witness to the unity that Christ prayed for, died for, and still longs to see fulfilled.

Closing Prayer

Lord Jesus Christ,
You are the Living Bread who came down from heaven,
the One who gave Yourself for the life of the world.
At Your table, You gather the scattered,
You heal the wounded,
and You make Your people one.

Forgive us, Lord,
for the times we have used Your table to divide rather than to reconcile,
to exclude rather than to embrace,
to defend our own boundaries rather than to proclaim Your boundless love.

Give us humble hearts, open hands,
and a renewed vision of Your Church —
as one Body, one Spirit,
called in one hope,
sharing one Bread and one Cup.

Make us one, Lord,
as You are one with the Father,
so that the world may believe
that You have been sent for its salvation.

To You, with the Father and the Holy Spirit,
be all glory, now and forever. Amen.

Chapter 9

Challenges to Eucharistic Unity

The call for **Eucharistic unity** stands at the heart of Christ's desire for His Church, yet it is one of the most difficult and complex challenges facing Christianity today. While the longing for unity burns deeply in the hearts of many believers, the path toward Eucharistic reconciliation is strewn with **theological disagreements**, **historic wounds**, and **pastoral dilemmas** that have shaped centuries of division.

These challenges are not trivial, nor are they merely matters of human stubbornness or misunderstanding. They touch upon profound questions of doctrine, sacramental theology, church order, and the faithfulness of the Church to Christ's commands. Can the Church remain true to the apostolic faith while seeking new paths of reconciliation? Can fidelity to theological integrity coexist with a bold openness to unity?

In this chapter, we will face these difficult questions head-on — not to offer simplistic solutions but to explore the real obstacles and the hopeful possibilities that lie before us as we seek to heal the divisions at Christ's table.

The Central Questions We Must Confront:

1- How can Christians overcome differences in Eucharistic theology?

   Throughout the Christian world, believers hold differing understandings of the nature of the Eucharist: Is Christ present literally, mystically, spiritually, or symbolically? These differences are not just academic — they shape how communities approach the altar and determine whom they welcome to the table.

2- **What role does apostolic succession play in Eucharistic validity?**

For many churches, particularly in Catholic and Orthodox traditions, the validity of the Eucharist depends on the unbroken line of ordination from the apostles. But can Christians from other traditions be fully united at the Eucharistic table without sharing this lineage?

3- **Can churches recognize each other's sacraments, especially baptism?**

Baptism is often seen as the gateway to Eucharistic participation, yet disputes over the mode, meaning, and recognition of baptism continue to divide Christian communities. Is it possible to move toward universal sacramental recognition, especially if we take St. Paul's declaration of "one Lord, one faith, one baptism" (Ephesians 4:5) seriously?

4- **How should church leaders approach the balance between fidelity to tradition and the call for unity?**

Priests, Pastors, bishops, and theologians face immense pastoral responsibility in this area. How can they guard the truths entrusted to them while also embodying the reconciling love of Christ? How can they lead their flocks toward unity without compromising the faith handed down to them?

What This Chapter Will Explore:

This chapter will examine these major challenges, walking carefully through the theological, historical, and pastoral issues that have kept Christians divided at the Lord's table. We will look at:

- **The doctrinal divergences** on Eucharistic theology, from transubstantiation to Memorialism.

- **The debates over apostolic succession** and what constitutes a valid Eucharist.

- **The problem of re-baptism** and the mutual recognition (or rejection) of sacraments across traditions.

- **The pastoral responsibility** of church leaders is to guide the people of God toward unity.

Throughout, we will listen attentively to Scripture, the early Church Fathers, and the living voices of today's Christian leaders, seeking not only to understand the challenges but to uncover signs of hope.

The Hope of Eucharistic Reconciliation:

The goal is not to erase real differences or to pretend that centuries of division can be overcome overnight. Rather, the goal is to open a space for **honest theological dialogue, mutual respect and shared longing for the unity that Christ Himself prayed for.**

Suppose we are to move toward Eucharistic reconciliation, we must be willing to engage these challenges with both **truth and love** — holding fast to the faith once delivered to the saints while also embracing the expansive mercy and hospitality of Christ, who gave His Body and Blood not to divide, but to unite.

May this chapter offer not only careful analysis but also a call to humility, repentance, and courageous hope as we seek together the healing of the Body of Christ.

1. Doctrinal Divergences on Eucharistic Theology

Perhaps the most significant and visible obstacle to Eucharistic communion among Christians today is the wide range of **theological interpretations** regarding the nature of the Eucharist itself. Across centuries and traditions, believers have asked:

- What exactly happens at the altar?
- How is Christ present in the bread and wine?
- Is the Eucharist a sacrifice, a memorial, or both?

These questions are not mere intellectual exercises — they lie at the heart of Christian worship and identity. They shape how each tradition approaches the Lord's Table and, importantly, whether it recognizes the Eucharistic practices of other churches as valid.

Key Views on the Eucharist Across Christian Traditions:

The varying interpretations have led to real, practical divisions in Christian life. For example:

- **Catholic and Orthodox Churches** insist on the real presence of Christ and see the Eucharist as a sacrificial offering, making intercommunion difficult with churches that understand it as a mere symbol.

- Many **Protestant traditions** emphasize the Eucharist as a commemorative or spiritual act, focusing on the believer's faith rather than the transformation of the elements.

- Even within Protestantism, differing views on Christ's presence have kept communities separated at the Lord's Table.

The Challenge: Divergent Understandings, Divided Tables

The result is that, across the Christian world, the Eucharist has become both a sign of grace and a marker of division. Instead of the **one bread and one cup** uniting all who confess Christ, we find separate altars, distinct theologies, and often mutual exclusion.

This is not how the early Church understood the Eucharist.

A Return to the Early Church's Perspective:

The early Church, while affirming the mystery of Christ's real presence, emphasized most of all the **unifying power of the Eucharist**.

St. Irenaeus of Lyons (2nd century) offers a beautiful image:

> "Just as the bread that is made from many grains becomes one loaf, so we, who are many, become one in Christ through the Eucharist" (*Against Heresies* 4.18.5).

For St. Irenaeus, the Eucharist was not just about what happened to the elements on the altar; it was about what happened to the people gathered around the altar. The Eucharist was the act that made the many into one Body, united in Christ.

St. Justin Martyr, another early Christian apologist, describes the Eucharistic celebration as a communal event centered on thanksgiving, prayer, and the shared reception of Christ's Body and Blood—not yet marked by the hardened theological categories that would develop in later centuries.

A Way Forward: Seeking Unity Without Erasing Differences

In light of these differences, can churches today find a way to respect one another's Eucharistic traditions without insisting on complete uniformity?

Several hopeful paths suggest themselves:

- **Focused theological dialogue** could clarify points of misunderstanding and highlight areas of genuine convergence. For example, even among traditions that reject transubstantiation, there is often deep reverence for Christ's presence and the sanctity of the Eucharist.

- **Shared liturgical experiences**—such as ecumenical prayer services or joint acts of thanksgiving—could build trust and relational bridges, even when formal intercommunion is not yet possible.

- **A renewed emphasis on the relational meaning of the Eucharist** — that it not only concerns what happens to the bread and wine but also what happens to the people who gather around the table — could re-center the conversation on Christ's unifying work.

Toward a Renewed Eucharistic Theology:

The goal is not to erase the real theological differences that exist nor to rush toward superficial unity. Rather, it is to ask:

- Can we focus on what **unites** rather than what divides?

- Can we allow the Eucharist to be not only a theological doctrine but also a relational and spiritual event, a moment of encounter where Christ draws us together?

- Can we approach one another with humility, willing to learn, to listen, and to discern where the Holy Spirit might be leading the Church in this generation?

Christ's Desire for Unity

We are reminded again of Christ's prayer on the night before His Passion:

"That they may all be one; even as You, Father, *are* in Me and I in You, that they also may be in Us, so that the world may believe that You sent Me" (John 17:21).

Restoring Eucharistic unity will require both **theological courage** and **spiritual humility**. It calls us not to compromise truth but to seek truth together, always with an eye toward the love that binds the Body of Christ.

As we continue to explore the other challenges to Eucharistic communion, may we carry forward the conviction that theological differences, while real and important, are not insurmountable barriers but potential opportunities for growth, dialogue, and greater unity in Christ.

2. Apostolic Succession and Its Role in Eucharistic Validity

Alongside differing Eucharistic theologies, one of the most significant—and often emotionally charged—obstacles to Eucharistic communion is the question of **apostolic succession**. For many churches, particularly in the Catholic, Orthodox, and some Anglican and Lutheran traditions, the validity of the Eucharist depends not only on the faith of the community but on the **lineage of ordination** that traces back to the apostles themselves.

But what does this doctrine mean, and how has it shaped the practice of Eucharistic inclusion or exclusion across Christian history?

What Is Apostolic Succession?

At its core, apostolic succession is the belief that Christ entrusted His authority to the apostles, who in turn passed it on through the laying on of hands to their successors—the bishops. This unbroken chain, safeguarded through episcopal ordination, is believed to guarantee not only the continuity of teaching but also the **validity of the sacraments**, especially the Eucharist.

"The one who listens to you listens to Me, and the one who rejects you rejects Me. And he who rejects Me rejects the One who sent Me" (Luke 10:16)

In this view, the authority to consecrate the Eucharist is not something any believer or minister can assume by personal calling or community affirmation; it is a gift handed down through the Church, safeguarded by apostolic lineage.

Different Views Across Traditions:

The importance placed on apostolic succession varies widely across Christian traditions. This divergence has profound practical consequences. The Catholic and Orthodox Churches, for example, do not officially recognize Protestant Eucharistic celebrations as valid because they believe Protestant ministers lack apostolic succession. Conversely, many Protestant traditions reject the need for historic episcopal succession, emphasizing instead the priesthood of all believers and the authority of Scripture.

The Challenge of Eucharistic Validity:

This disagreement creates real barriers:

- Catholic and Orthodox Christians often cannot share the Eucharist with Protestant Christians because they do not recognize Protestant clergy as having the authority to consecrate the Body and Blood of Christ.

- Protestant communities may not accept Catholic or Orthodox claims that apostolic succession is essential, believing that faith in Christ and the community's intention to remember Him are sufficient.

- Even within traditions that affirm apostolic succession (such as Catholic and Orthodox), mutual recognition has sometimes been strained or suspended due to schism or doctrinal disagreement.

The Witness of the Church Fathers

While apostolic succession was emphasized in the early Church as a safeguard of right teaching and sacramental life, the Fathers also consistently emphasized that the heart of the Church's unity is **Christ Himself**.

St. Augustine writes:

> "Let us seek Christ in the Eucharist, and let us seek Him in one another, for in both He is truly present" (*Sermon 272*).

Is There a Path to Greater Recognition?

While differences over apostolic succession are real and rooted in long-standing theological convictions, there may be pastoral and theological pathways to greater mutual understanding:

- **Recognizing each other's ministries without compromising core convictions**: Is it possible to affirm the integrity and faithfulness of Christian communities even when formal apostolic succession is not shared?

- **Exploring a broader theology of Eucharistic presence**: Could dialogue across traditions open space to appreciate how Christ acts in diverse Eucharistic contexts, even when understandings of ordination differ?

- **Fostering pastoral sensitivity and humility**: Church leaders can work toward unity by emphasizing what is shared—faith in Christ, baptism, Scripture—while respectfully acknowledging unresolved differences.

Reflection:

- How can we balance the importance of apostolic succession with a commitment to Christian unity?

- Are there ways to recognize the presence of Christ in the Eucharistic celebrations of other traditions without denying the value of apostolic continuity?

- How can church leaders and theologians foster dialogue and mutual respect around this sensitive issue, helping the faithful avoid attitudes of superiority or exclusion?

Toward Greater Eucharistic Reconciliation

Apostolic succession will remain an important theological question as the Church seeks unity, but it must not become an **absolute barrier** that ignores the deeper work of the Spirit across the Body of Christ. As we explore the next challenge—how baptismal recognition shapes Eucharistic sharing—let us carry forward a spirit of humility, charity, and longing for the unity Christ prayed for.

3. The Issue of Re-Baptism and Recognition of Sacraments

Beyond Eucharistic theology and apostolic succession, another major obstacle to Eucharistic unity is the question of

sacramental recognition, particularly regarding **baptism**. Baptism is the gateway to the Christian life and the foundation of sacramental participation. In that case, divisions over its recognition inevitably affect whether Christians from different traditions can approach the Eucharistic table together.

At its heart, this issue raises deeply pastoral and theological questions:

- What makes a baptism valid?

- Must one be rebaptized when moving between Christian traditions?

- How do divergent understandings of baptismal practice shape our capacity to recognize one another as part of the one Body of Christ?

The Problem of Re-Baptism

Historically, some churches have required **rebaptism** for Christians entering their fellowship, often based on doubts about the validity of the baptism they previously received.

- The **Catholic Church** generally recognizes the baptisms of other churches if they were performed with water and in the name of the Father, Son, and Holy Spirit, but it does not recognize baptisms from groups it deems non-Trinitarian (such as Jehovah's Witnesses or Mormons).

- The **Orthodox Churches** vary in practice: some recognize Catholic baptisms, while others may require a form of rebaptism or chrismation (anointing with oil) for full reception.

- Many **Protestant churches** practice **conditional rebaptism**, particularly if the original baptism was performed on infants or not by immersion, reflecting a conviction that baptism must be a conscious act of faith.

This fragmentation has led to situations where Christians are told, explicitly or implicitly, that their baptism "does not count" outside their original tradition. Such practices reinforce division and raise profound theological questions about the meaning of "one baptism."

What Does Scripture Teach?

St. Paul's teaching in Ephesians speaks directly to the unity of the Christian body grounded in baptism:

> "There is one body and one Spirit, just as also you were called in one hope of your calling; one Lord, one faith, one baptism; one God and Father of all who is over all and through all and in all" (Ephesians 4:4–6).

If there is **one baptism**, then the Church is called to recognize its fundamental unity across traditions, even when liturgical expressions or theological emphases differ. Baptism is not the possession of a single denomination or tradition; it is the sacramental entry into the universal Body of Christ.

The Witness of the Church Fathers:

St. Cyprian of Carthage (3rd century) famously engaged in debates over the recognition of baptisms performed by heretics. While he advocated rebaptism, many of his contemporaries, including the bishop of Rome, argued that baptism, once performed in the name of the Trinity, need not be repeated.

St. Cyprian's statement remains challenging and provocative:

> "As Christ is one, so too must His baptism be one, and His Eucharist be one" (*Epistle 73:21*).

For St. Cyprian, the unity of baptism was inseparably linked to the unity of the Eucharist. Divided baptismal practices fracture the visible unity that should be manifested at the Lord's Table.

Toward a Path of Greater Recognition

In today's ecumenical landscape, many churches are exploring ways to overcome this obstacle:

- **Agreements on baptismal recognition**: The Catholic Church, Orthodox Churches, and many mainline Protestant churches are now formally considering recognizing each other's baptisms, provided they are Trinitarian and performed with water.

- **Ecumenical documents** such as the *Baptism, Eucharist, and Ministry* (BEM) text produced by the World Council of Churches have helped clarify shared understandings and map out areas of ongoing disagreement.

- **Dialogue on sacramental theology** continues to explore how differences in emphasis (such as believer's baptism vs. infant baptism) can be held in tension without excluding one another from Eucharistic fellowship.

A Way Forward

What steps could help remove baptismal disputes as a barrier to Eucharistic unity?

- Churches could **affirm a common standard for baptism** rooted in Scripture and the early Church: water baptism performed in the name of the Father, Son, and Holy Spirit.

- Christian communities could emphasize baptism as a **sign of incorporation into Christ**, not merely a denominational badge or theological declaration.

- Greater pastoral sensitivity could help avoid practices that humiliate or invalidate the Christian journey of those seeking to enter a new tradition.

As **St. Paul** reminds us:

> "For also by one Spirit we were all baptized into one body, whether Jews or Greeks, whether slaves or free, and we were all made to drink of one Spirit" (1 Corinthians 12:13).

The Eucharist, which nourishes the one Body of Christ, must be built on the shared foundation of baptism that unites believers across every human divide.

Reflection:

- Are we, as Christians, honoring the unity of baptism in our practices, or are we using baptismal differences to reinforce separation?

- How can churches foster **mutual recognition of sacraments** without compromising theological convictions?

- What pastoral practices might help Christians experience baptism as a source of unity, not division, preparing the way for greater Eucharistic reconciliation?

As we prepare to examine the role of pastoral leadership in guiding the Church toward unity, let us remember that Christ has already given His Church the foundation: one baptism into one Body, nourished at one table, for the glory of one Lord.

4. The Pastoral Responsibility of Church Leaders in Guiding Unity

While theological disagreements and sacramental divergences create formidable barriers to Eucharistic communion, it is ultimately the responsibility of **pastoral leaders** — bishops, priests, pastors, elders, theologians, and ecumenical leaders — to navigate these complexities with wisdom, humility, and love.

The call to unity is not a theoretical exercise; it is a lived, relational, and sacramental vocation entrusted by Christ to His shepherds for the good of the entire Body of Christ.

> "I do not ask on behalf of these alone, but for those also who believe in Me through their word; that they may all be one; even as You, Father, are in Me and I in You, that they also may be in Us, so that the world may believe that You sent Me" (John 17:20-21).

These words from Christ's High Priestly Prayer place a profound responsibility on the Church's leaders—not only to safeguard doctrine but to lead the people of God into the unity that reflects the love and communion of God Himself.

Church Leaders as Stewards of Unity:

Throughout the New Testament, the call for unity resounds as a pastoral imperative:

St. Paul exhorts the Philippians:

> "Fulfill my joy, that you think the same *way,* by maintaining the same love, *being* united in spirit, thinking on one purpose" (Philippians 2:2).

St. Peter urges humility and shepherding:

> "Shepherd the flock of God among you, overseeing not under compulsion, but willingly, according to God; and not for dishonest gain, but with eagerness" (1 Peter 5:2).

St. Paul challenges the Corinthians over their divisions:

> "Has Christ been divided? Was Paul crucified for you? Or were you baptized in the name of Paul?" (1 Corinthians 1:13).

The unity of the Church is not merely a pastoral preference; it is a pastoral **duty**. Leaders are called to be bridge-builders, not wall-erectors; reconcilers, not mere custodians of institutional boundaries.

The Challenge of Balancing Fidelity and Openness:

Of course, pastoral responsibility is never a simple matter of ignoring differences or sacrificing truth for superficial unity. Leaders must hold together two essential tensions:

- **Fidelity to tradition**: safeguarding the apostolic faith, the integrity of sacramental life, and the Church's theological identity.

- **Openness to reconciliation**: working tirelessly for healing, dialogue, and new pathways of communion, even across longstanding divides.

This tension requires discernment, courage, and a deep trust in the guidance of the Holy Spirit.

Pastoral Approaches for Greater Eucharistic Unity:

Here are some concrete ways pastoral leaders can embody this responsibility:

1- **Encouraging Dialogue**: Bishops, priests, pastors, and theologians must engage one another across denominational lines—not merely to debate or defend positions, but to listen, learn, and seek common ground. Ecumenical dialogues, joint theological commissions, and shared study projects offer essential spaces where understanding can grow.

2- **Promoting Common Worship and Prayer**: Even when formal intercommunion is not yet possible, **shared prayer services, ecumenical liturgies, and common acts of witness** can build relational and spiritual bridges. These gatherings remind the faithful that unity is already present in baptism, Scripture, and shared discipleship—and that the Eucharistic table remains a goal toward which we journey together.

3- **Fostering Love Over Legalism**: Pastoral leaders must continually ask: Are we protecting the Eucharist in ways that honor Christ, or are we reinforcing human divisions? Are our rules and exclusions drawing people toward holiness and reconciliation, or are they becoming barriers to the very grace Christ offers?

Reflection:

- How can pastoral leaders today balance the **integrity of their own traditions** with the call to build unity across denominational lines?

- What concrete actions could be taken in local churches to promote **Eucharistic reconciliation**, even in small and gradual ways?

- Are there places where pastoral attitudes or policies need to shift from **defensiveness** to **openness**, from **guarding boundaries** to **healing divisions**?

A Shepherding Vision for Unity:

Ultimately, the pastoral responsibility for Eucharistic unity is not about surrendering theological convictions or erasing historical identities. It is about **leading the people of God**

toward the unity Christ desires by shepherding them wisely, humbly, and lovingly toward the Table where He offers Himself to make them one.

As we prepare to close this chapter, we turn to the broader call to overcome divisions—not as an abstract theological project but as a lived, sacramental, and pastoral commitment to the healing of Christ's Body.

Conclusion: The Call to Overcome Divisions

Throughout this chapter, we have walked carefully through some of the most pressing and painful obstacles to Eucharistic communion:

- The **doctrinal divergences** in Eucharistic theology shape how different traditions understand the mystery of Christ's presence.

- The debates over **apostolic succession** and what constitutes the valid celebration of the Eucharist.

- The struggles surrounding **the recognition of sacraments**, especially baptism, which should unite believers but has too often divided them.

- The profound **pastoral responsibility** borne by Church leaders to guide the faithful toward unity with both fidelity and courage.

Each of these challenges carries a long history of wounds, debates, and entrenched convictions. And yet, if we listen carefully—not only to the voices of history and theology but to the voice of Christ Himself—we are confronted with an unmistakable summons:

> "That they may all be one; even as You, Father, *are* in Me and I in You, that they also may be in Us, so that the world may believe that You sent Me" (John 17:21).

Eucharistic unity is not a marginal issue, nor is it merely a technical or institutional matter. It stands at the very heart of the Church's vocation to bear witness to the Gospel. When Christians gather at separate tables, refusing to break bread together, the world sees a divided Christ. When we remain locked in our own traditions without seeking reconciliation, we betray the unity for which Christ gave His life.

A Path Forward:

The road to Eucharistic reconciliation will not be quick, and it will not be easy. It will require:

1- **Theological dialogue** that is honest, rigorous, and open to the movement of the Holy Spirit.

2- **Pastoral creativity** finds new ways for Christians to pray, serve, and journey together.

3- **Spiritual humility** places love above pride, mercy above defensiveness, and Christ's will above human control.

This is not to say that all differences will disappear, nor that the Church should pursue unity at the expense of truth. Rather, it is to say that unity is **God's gift and calling**—and that we are responsible for cooperating with His reconciling work.

> "Therefore, accept one another, just as Christ also accepted us to the glory of God" (Romans 15:7).

The Challenge to the Church Today:

The challenge is clear:

- Will we allow doctrinal disagreements, historical grievances, and ecclesiastical boundaries to continue dividing the Body of Christ at His table?

- Or will we, with humility and courage, seek to overcome these barriers—trusting that the same Christ who gives Himself in the Eucharist can also unite His people through it?

Unity does not mean uniformity. It means learning to see Christ in one another, to recognize His work across traditions, and to trust that He is leading His Church toward the fulfillment of His prayer.

A Final Exhortation:

Let us hear again the words of **St. Paul**:

> "There is one body and one Spirit, just as also you were called in one hope of your calling; one Lord, one faith, one baptism; one God and Father of all who is over all and through all and in all" (Ephesians 4:4-6).

If we are one Body, called by one Lord, baptized into one faith, then we must find a way—by God's grace—to come together at one table.

Let the Eucharist no longer be the symbol of our division but the sacrament of our reconciliation. Let it be not the prize of the righteous but the healing gift of the One who gave His Body to make us whole.

May the Church rise to this challenge—not for its own sake, but so that the world may see and believe in the love of the Father, the sacrifice of the Son, and the unity wrought by the Spirit.

Reflection: A Heart Turned Toward Eucharistic Reconciliation

As we come to the end of this chapter, we are left with both a burden and a hope. The burden is the heavy weight of Christian division—the pain of separated communities, divided tables, and long-standing mistrust. We cannot deny the deep theological, historical, and pastoral challenges that stand in the way of Eucharistic unity. To pretend otherwise would be dishonest.

Yet alongside this burden is a profound hope—the hope that Christ Himself is still at work in His Church, that the Holy Spirit has not ceased calling us toward reconciliation, and that the Eucharist we celebrate, even when fragmented, remains a living sign of the unity we are called to embrace.

The work of overcoming division is not only a theological project or an institutional goal. It is a matter of the heart.

- Are we willing to let our hearts be broken by the divisions in Christ's Body?

- Are we ready to pray, not just for our own traditions but for the healing of the whole Church?

- Are we prepared to lay down pride, suspicion, or fear and step forward in humility toward the unity that Christ desires?

This is not easy work, but it is holy work. It is work that belongs to all Christians—not only bishops or theologians but every member of the Body who hungers for the fullness of Christ's presence and the reconciliation of His people.

As we pray now, let us entrust this longing to the One who gave Himself for the life of the world, asking Him to unite what we have divided and to lead us, step by step, toward the table of perfect love.

Closing Prayer

Lord Jesus Christ,
You are the Bread of Life,
broken for the healing of the nations,
poured out for the reconciliation of all creation.

We stand before You today as a divided people,
grieving the fractures in Your Body,
aching for the day when all who love You
may gather at one table,
sharing one Bread, drinking one Cup,
and proclaiming one faith.

Forgive us, Lord,
for the ways we have deepened division
through pride, fear, or indifference.
Forgive us for treating Your Eucharist,
as a possession to be guarded
rather than a gift to be shared.

Pour out Your Spirit upon Your Church, O Lord.
Soften hardened hearts, open closed doors,
and lead us on the path of truth and love.
Strengthen pastors, theologians, and leaders.
to guide Your people with wisdom and courage.
Raise up in all of us a longing for unity
that reflects the unity You share with the Father,
so that the world may believe in Your saving love.

We entrust this prayer to You,
with trust in Your mercy and faith in Your promises,
for You live and reign with the Father and the Holy Spirit,
one God, forever and ever. Amen.

Chapter 10

An Invitation to the Lord's Table

The Eucharist is **Christ's gift to His Church**—not a mere ritual, not an abstract symbol, but the living, transformative presence of His Body and Blood, offered to nourish, heal, and unite His people. It is the great sacrament of unity, binding believers not only to Christ but also to one another, making them one Body through the one Bread and one Cup.

Yet, for centuries, Christians have found themselves divided at the very table that was meant to bring them together.

- Catholics, Orthodox, and Protestants gather in separate sanctuaries.

- Denominations erect boundaries around the altar, limiting access and recognition.

- Historic wounds, doctrinal disputes, and mutual suspicions keep believers apart, even as they all proclaim faith in the same Lord.

This painful contradiction between the **oneness Christ desires** and the **separation we perpetuate** is perhaps the deepest wound in the heart of the Church today.

> "Since there is one bread, we who are many are one body, for we all partake of the one bread" (1 Corinthians 10:17).

If the Eucharist is truly the Body and Blood of Christ, then every Christian who loves the Lord should long for a path toward Eucharistic communion — not as a compromise of truth, but as a fulfillment of Christ's prayer for His people.

What This Chapter Will Explore:

This chapter is not merely a theological discussion; it is **a heartfelt invitation** — a call to all Christians to return, together, to the Lord's Table. We will explore four key themes that shape this invitation:

1. **Overcoming Barriers to Eucharistic Communion Through Dialogue and Love:**

   How can believers address the real and painful divisions that keep them apart at the altar, not by ignoring truth but by engaging in dialogue marked by love and humility?

2. **The Role of Church Leaders in Leading Toward Unity:**

   What responsibility do bishops, priests, pastors, and theologians bear in shepherding the Church toward Eucharistic reconciliation? How can they guide their flocks with courage, wisdom, and pastoral care?

3. **A Plea to All Christian Churches to Come Together at the Altar:**

   This is not only the work of leaders or theologians; it is the shared longing and responsibility of every Christian community. How can the global Church hear and respond to Christ's urgent desire that His followers be one?

4- **The Power of Eucharistic Participation in Transforming Hearts and Minds:**

The Eucharist is not only a sign of unity; it is the means by which Christ transforms His people into one Body. How can recovering the centrality and meaning of the Eucharist heal divisions and renew Christian witness in the world?

The Urgency of This Moment:

This chapter comes with a sense of urgency. The divisions among Christians are not only theological or institutional; they are a wound in the witness of the Church before a watching world.

- How can we preach reconciliation while remaining unreconciled at the altar?

- How can we proclaim one Gospel while living as though we are many gospels, many bodies, many tables?

The invitation is clear: Christ is calling His people to return — not merely to the forms of religion, but to the heart of faith, where He gives Himself fully and freely in the Eucharist.

This is an invitation to repentance, to dialogue, to healing, and to hope. It is an invitation to let Christ's Body and Blood, offered for the life of the world, become once again the great sign and instrument of unity among all who bear His name.

As we journey through this chapter, may we open our hearts to hear this call—not as a distant ideal or a theological debate, but as a living invitation from the Lord Himself, who sets His table before us and says:

> Now, while they were eating, Jesus took some bread, and after a blessing, He broke it. And giving it to the disciples, He said, "Take, eat; this is My body." And when He had taken a cup and given thanks, He gave it to them, saying, "Drink from it, all of you; for this is My blood of the covenant, which is poured out for many for the forgiveness of sins" (Matthew 26:26-28).

- The Table of the Lord is set.

- Will we come together?

1. Overcoming Barriers to Eucharistic Unity

The barriers that divide Christians at the Eucharistic table are real, deep, and often painful. They are not mere misunderstandings or surface-level disagreements; they reach into the heart of Christian identity, theology, and practice. Yet the Gospel we proclaim is a Gospel of reconciliation—reconciliation between humanity and God and reconciliation between brothers and sisters in Christ.

> "For He Himself is our peace, who made both *groups* one and broke down the dividing wall of the partition" (Ephesians 2:14).

If we truly believe in the power of Christ to overcome sin, heal divisions, and unite His people, then we must believe that no theological or historical barrier is beyond the reach of His grace.

Identifying the Barriers:

Before we can overcome the barriers, we must name them honestly and humbly:

1- **Theological Differences**: Disagreements over the nature of the Eucharist, the meaning of the real presence, the theology of the priesthood, and the sacrificial character of the Mass.

2- **Historical Wounds**: The scars left by centuries of division—such as the Great Schism between East and West (1054), the Protestant Reformation (1517), and countless subsequent splits—have left deep mistrust and entrenched separation.

3- **Ecclesial Exclusivism**: The conviction held by many traditions that only they possess the true Eucharist, the valid ministry, or the correct doctrine often leads to the exclusion of others from Eucharistic sharing.

These are not trivial obstacles. They are the result of real convictions and painful histories. But the question remains: **How can we begin to move beyond them?**

How Do We Overcome These Barriers?

Dialogue Rooted in Love:

Theological conversations cannot simply be debates where each side tries to win or defend its position. True dialogue must be grounded in love—a love for Christ and a love for one another that prioritizes reconciliation over victory.

> "By this, all will know that you are My disciples, if you have love for one another" (John 13:35).

This kind of dialogue requires humility, patience, and the willingness to listen—not only to defend one's own tradition but to understand and honor the convictions of others.

Recognition of Christ in One Another:

If we believe that Christ is truly present in the Eucharist, we must also believe that He is present in those who love Him, even across denominational lines. We cannot claim to recognize Christ on the altar while failing to recognize Him in the faces of our brothers and sisters.

> "And this commandment we have from Him, that the one who loves God should love his brother also" (1 John 4:21).

This recognition does not erase differences, but it calls us to approach one another with reverence, charity, and hope.

1- Healing Historical Wounds:

The divisions of the past cannot be undone, but they can be healed. Healing begins with repentance—acknowledging the sins and failures that contributed to division—and with forgiveness, extended across the boundaries of history and tradition.

As the Church commits to reconciliation, it must walk a path of **renewal**:

- Renewing its commitment to Christ's mission.

- Renewing its openness to the Holy Spirit's work.

- Renewing its relationships across ecclesial lines.

The Example of the Early Church:

In the earliest days of the Christian community, unity was not an abstract goal but a lived reality centered on the breaking of bread:

> "And they were continually devoting themselves to the apostles' teaching and to the fellowship, to the breaking of bread and to the prayers" (Acts 2:42).

Even as the Church faced challenges, tensions, and persecutions, the Eucharist remained the center of its unity, a visible sign that believers were one body in Christ.

St. Paul reminds the Corinthians:

> "Is not the cup of blessing which we bless a sharing in the blood of Christ? Is not the bread which we break a sharing in the body of Christ? 17 Since there is one bread, we who are many are one body, for we all partake of the one bread" (1 Corinthians 10:16–17).

The Eucharist was never meant to be the prize for perfect agreement but the means by which imperfect believers are drawn together, forgiven, and made one.

A Vision from St. John Chrysostom:

The great preacher of the early Church, **St. John Chrysostom**, captured the transcendent mystery of the Eucharist:

> "When you see the Lord immolated and lying on the altar, and the priest standing over the sacrifice praying, and all the people empurpled by that precious blood, can you think you are still among men and on earth? Are you not lifted to Heaven?" (*Homily on the Eucharist*).

If the Eucharist lifts us to Heaven, how can we allow earthly divisions to keep us apart? If we are gathered before the Lamb of God, how can we cling to the walls we have built on earth?

Reflection:

- Are we willing to engage in dialogue marked by humility and love?

- Can we learn to see Christ not only in the sacrament but in one another?

- Are we ready to seek healing for the historical wounds that continue to divide Christ's Body?

A Step Toward the Table:

Overcoming barriers to Eucharistic communion is not a quick or simple task. But it begins here: with a commitment to dialogue, to love, to recognition, and healing. It begins with the conviction that Christ's desire for unity is stronger than our divisions—and that, by His grace, the Church can find its way back to the table where He waits to make us one.

2. The Role of Church Leaders in Leading Toward Unity

While the call to Eucharistic unity belongs to the whole Church, **the weight of responsibility** falls in a particular way upon those entrusted with leadership. Bishops, priests, pastors, theologians, elders, and ecumenical leaders are the stewards of Christ's flock. They have been charged not only with safeguarding doctrine but also with fostering communion, healing divisions, and guiding the people of God toward the unity that Christ Himself prayed for.

> "Shepherd the flock of God among you, overseeing not under compulsion, but willingly, according to God; and not for dishonest gain, but with eagerness; nor yet as lording it over those allotted to you, but being examples to the flock" (1 Peter 5:2-3).

True Christian leadership is marked by humility, wisdom, and love—not domination or control. And when it comes to the sensitive and complex matter of Eucharistic reconciliation, this kind of leadership is indispensable.

Why Leadership Matters:

The divisions that separate Christians at the Eucharistic table are often reinforced and perpetuated by institutional structures and theological positions that only leaders can address.

- **It is bishops, synods, councils, and theological commissions** that set official policies on intercommunion, sacramental recognition, and ecumenical engagement.

- **It is pastors, priests, and ministers** who model for their congregations how to view believers from other traditions—with suspicion or with charity, with hostility or with hope.

- **It is theologians and teachers** who shape how the faithful understand the meaning of the Eucharist, the nature of the Church, and the path toward unity.

Without courageous and faithful leadership, the Church risks remaining locked in patterns of isolation and division.

How Can Church Leaders Foster Eucharistic Unity?

1. Encouraging Theological Dialogue

Church leaders must take the initiative to engage one another across denominational boundaries—not merely defending their own positions but seeking common ground and opening space for the Holy Spirit to work.

Formal dialogues between churches can clarify misunderstandings, explore theological differences, and identify shared convictions.

Joint study commissions can examine historical disputes in a new light, asking whether past disagreements still apply or whether reconciliation is now possible.

Shared declarations on core matters of faith can pave the way for closer Eucharistic fellowship.

> "Being diligent to keep the unity of the Spirit in the bond of peace. There is one body and one Spirit, just as also you were called in one hope of your calling" (Ephesians 4:3–4).

2. Promoting Common Prayer and Worship:

While full Eucharistic sharing may not yet be possible in many contexts, leaders can promote **common prayer services, ecumenical liturgies, and joint acts of service** as powerful signs of unity in Christ.

Gathering together in prayer opens hearts to one another and reminds the faithful that they already share much in common.

Collaborative service projects can build trust, friendship, and mutual respect, preparing the ground for deeper sacramental unity.

3. Prioritizing Love Over Legalism:

Church leaders must always balance doctrinal fidelity with pastoral compassion. There are times when rules, boundaries, and safeguards are necessary to protect the integrity of the Church's faith. But there are also times when **legalism hardens hearts** and **blocks the work of grace**.

- Are our policies around the Eucharist protecting the holiness of the sacrament—or are they reinforcing human divisions?

- Are we acting as faithful shepherds or as gatekeepers more focused on institutional control than on Christ's reconciling love?

Leaders are called to **merciful, inclusive spirit** — showing the faithful how to approach one another with generosity, humility, and hope.

Historical Examples of Courageous Leadership:

Throughout Church history, moments of reconciliation and healing have often been led by courageous pastors and bishops who were willing to cross boundaries and extend hands of friendship.

In the early centuries, bishops like **St. Irenaeus of Lyons** worked tirelessly to preserve unity in the face of theological conflict, reminding the faithful that the Church's center is Christ Himself.

In the modern era, **ecumenical pioneers** have taken concrete steps to mend old rifts and open pathways of renewed dialogue.

Today, countless local leaders quietly build bridges across denominational lines through shared prayer, dialogue, and acts of love.

These examples remind us that leadership for unity is not only the work of popes, patriarchs, or global councils — it is the calling of every shepherd who longs to see Christ's people reconciled.

Reflection:

- Are today's Church leaders willing to take risks for the sake of unity, or have they become too comfortable with the status quo?

- How can local pastors and priests foster a spirit of ecumenical openness in their communities, even before formal intercommunion is possible?

- Are we, as the people of God, praying for our leaders — asking the Holy Spirit to give them wisdom, courage, and love in guiding the Church toward reconciliation?

The Shepherds' Sacred Task:

The call to Eucharistic unity is not optional. It is written into the very fabric of the Gospel, entrusted to those called to shepherd Christ's flock.

As we move into the next section — a plea for all Christian churches to come together at the altar — let us remember: the healing of the Church's divisions will depend not only on good theology but on holy, humble, and courageous leadership that dares to follow the Good Shepherd Himself.

3. A Plea to All Christian Churches to Come Together at the Altar

At the heart of the Gospel lies Christ's passionate desire for His people to be one. On the night before His death, in His final, intimate prayer to the Father, the Lord Jesus did not pray for institutional success, doctrinal perfection, or worldly triumph. He prayed for unity.

"I do not ask on behalf of these alone, but for those also who believe in Me through their word; that they may all be one; even as You, Father, are in Me and I in You, that they also may be in Us, so that the world may believe that You sent Me" (John 17:20-21).

Christian unity is not merely a polite ideal or an optional theological bonus—it is the very heart of Christ's mission. And the greatest sign of this unity is the gathering of believers at the Eucharistic table, where Christ gives Himself fully to His people and makes them one Body in Him.

The Pain of Our Divisions:

Yet we must face the painful reality:

- We proclaim one Lord, but we gather at many altars.

- We preach one baptism, but we defend separate tables.

- We are called to be one Body, but we often live as divided parts, suspicious of one another, hesitant to embrace and slow to reconcile.

This is not simply a matter of theology or ecclesiastical protocol. It is a wound in the Body of Christ. It is a scandal before the world. It is a contradiction of the very Eucharist we claim to celebrate.

"Is Christ divided?" (1 Corinthians 1:13)

An Urgent Plea to the Churches:

In light of this, we raise a plea—a heartfelt call to all Christian churches, across traditions and histories, to hear the invitation of the Lord and move toward reconciliation at His table.

To the Catholic and Orthodox Churches:

You hold in your hands the treasure of apostolic succession, the living memory of the early Church, and a profound reverence for the mystery of the Eucharist. Will you lead the way in seeking Eucharistic unity—not demanding that all theological issues be solved before fellowship can begin, but opening the door to dialogue, shared worship, and incremental steps toward communion?

To the Protestant Churches:

You have cherished the primacy of Scripture, the necessity of personal faith, and the power of grace. Can you rediscover the Eucharist not merely as a symbolic memorial but as a real, transformative encounter with the living Christ—a means through which He draws His people together in love and truth?

To All Christian Believers:

We are all part of this broken and scattered Body. Will we pray, work, and hope for the day when we will again break bread together at the same altar? Will we commit to lives of repentance, humility, and courageous love, seeking the unity that Christ commands?

The Witness of St. Augustine:

St. Augustine, who lived in a time of fierce division, understood that receiving the Eucharist is not only a personal act—it is a commitment to unity with others.

> "Recognize in the bread what hung on the Cross, and in the cup what flowed from His side. If you receive it, you must also be one in heart and spirit with those who share it" (*Sermon 272*).

Receiving Christ's Body requires that we also embrace one another as members of His Body. The Eucharist is not only vertical, connecting us to God; it is horizontal, binding us to one another.

A Call to Conversion:

This plea is not a naïve call to erase differences overnight. It is a call to conversion.

- Conversion from suspicion to trust.

- Conversion from isolation to dialogue.

- Conversion from pride to humility.

- Conversion from division to reconciliation.

This is the work of the Holy Spirit—not human effort alone. But the Spirit moves most powerfully where hearts are open, where leaders are courageous, and where believers are willing to walk the long road toward unity.

Reflection:

- How can each Christian tradition take practical steps toward healing the divisions that separate us at the altar?

- What would it look like for local communities to pray regularly for Eucharistic unity, not only in formal settings but in the quiet longing of their hearts?

- Are we willing to let go of old hurts, hardened assumptions, or defensive postures in order to respond to Christ's call to oneness?

A Vision of Hope:

We believe in a God who raises the dead. We believe in a Christ who breaks down every dividing wall. We believe in a Spirit who makes all things new.

The plea to come together at the altar is not wishful thinking—it is a bold act of hope grounded in the unshakable promise of Christ. As we move forward, let us carry this hope with humility and determination, trusting that the unity Christ prayed for is not only His will but His sure and certain future for His Church.

4. The Power of Eucharistic Participation in Transforming Hearts and Minds

The Eucharist is not merely a ritual or theological concept—it is an encounter. When believers gather at the altar to partake of the Body and Blood of Christ, they are drawn into the deepest mystery of God's love and into the transformative work of His grace.

This is why the Eucharist holds such profound power, not only for the individual soul but for the Church as a whole. Through the Eucharist, God can heal divisions, soften hardened hearts, and renew minds because it is nothing less than **Christ Himself given for us**.

> "He who eats My flesh and drinks My blood abides in Me, and I in him" (John 6:56).

In every true Eucharistic celebration, Christ is present—not only on the altar but within His people, shaping them into His likeness and knitting them together as His Body.

What Happens When We Receive the Eucharist?

What Happens When We Receive the Eucharist?

The Eucharist is not merely a ritual or symbolic remembrance; it is a profound mystery of communion, transformation, and mission. Through this holy sacrament, God draws us into the very heart of His divine life, binding us not only to Christ but also to one another and sending us forth as His living presence in the world. Let us explore what truly happens when we approach the Eucharistic table with faith.

We Become One with Christ:

When we receive the Eucharist, we are not simply partaking in bread and wine; we are participating in the life of Christ Himself. Through the sacred mystery of the altar, we are drawn into His death and resurrection. We are invited to share in His victory over sin and death, to receive His grace, and to be filled with His Holy Spirit.

As St. Paul writes, "The one who joins himself to the Lord is one spirit *with Him*" (1 Corinthians 6:17). This means that Eucharistic communion is not a distant or symbolic connection — it is an intimate, personal union. We are united to Christ as the branches are to the vine, drawing life, nourishment, and strength from Him (John 15:5). This living union is the very foundation of Christian life, shaping not only our relationship with God but also empowering our mission in the world.

Through the Eucharist, Christ shares Himself entirely with us: His body broken, His blood poured out, His Spirit given — so that we might be transformed into His likeness, healed, forgiven, renewed, and made alive in Him.

We Become One with One Another:

The Eucharist is never a private affair. Even when we come to the altar individually, we receive something that binds us into a larger reality: the communion of the Church. As we partake of the one Bread, we become one Body; as we drink from the one Cup, we are united in the one Spirit.

Paul reminds the Corinthians, "Since there is one bread, we who are many are one body, for we all partake of the one bread" (1 Corinthians 10:17). This Eucharistic unity breaks down the barriers that divide us — whether of race, nationality, social class, or denomination. At the foot of the cross and the table of the Lord, we are no longer many scattered individuals but are knit together into the one Body of Christ.

In this sacred communion, the Church's unity is not something we achieve by our own effort; it is a gift Christ has already established, and the Holy Spirit makes visible and real through the Eucharist. Every Eucharistic celebration is thus both a sign and a means of healing the wounds of division and calling us to live out the unity we profess.

We Become the Body of Christ in the World:

Yet the transformation of the Eucharist does not end at the altar. Those who are fed at the Eucharistic table are sent out into the world to be Christ's presence — His hands, His feet, His voice, His heart. The Eucharist commissions the Church to become an agent of reconciliation, justice, mercy, and love.

As Paul writes, "Now you are Christ's body, and individually members of it" (1 Corinthians 12:27). This is not merely a spiritual metaphor but a concrete calling. Through the Eucharistic mystery, God shapes the Church's identity and mission: those who Christ has nourished must now nourish others; those who have received peace must now bring peace; those who have encountered mercy must now extend mercy.

In this way, the Eucharist becomes the wellspring of Christian witness. Through it, we are not only drawn closer to Christ and each other, but we are also propelled outward to be His ambassadors in a fractured world — signs of hope, agents of unity, and instruments of His transforming love.

The Healing Power of the Eucharist:

Through Eucharistic participation, God can transform not only individuals but also communities and even longstanding divisions within the Church.

1- **Healing of Divisions**: When Christians from different backgrounds share in Christ's Body and Blood, barriers of suspicion, pride, and misunderstanding can begin to fall.

2- **Renewed Love for One Another**: Eucharistic communion fosters compassion, humility, and forgiveness, calling believers to see each other not as rivals but as beloved members of the same Body.

3- **A Foretaste of the Heavenly Banquet**: The Eucharist is an anticipation of the final unity we will share in the Kingdom of God, where all the redeemed will gather at the marriage supper of the Lamb.

> "Blessed are those who are invited to the marriage supper [wedding feast] of the Lamb" (Revelation 19:9).

The Voice of St. Cyril of Jerusalem:

St. Cyril of Jerusalem, teaching the newly baptized in the fourth century, urged them to approach the Eucharist with faith and joy:

> "Do not approach with doubt, but with faith. Take, eat, and rejoice. For in this meal, Christ makes you one with Himself and with His people" (*Mystagogical Catecheses* 5).

The Eucharist is not just bread and wine—it is the divine means through which the Holy Spirit transforms our hearts, unites His Church, and renews the world.

Reflection:

- Are we approaching the Eucharist with the expectation that God, through Christ and by the Holy Spirit, will truly transform us?

- Are we allowing the grace of the Eucharist to shape how we see and treat fellow Christians across denominational lines?

- Are we ready to become not only receivers but also **witnesses** of the reconciling power of Christ in the world?

A Call to Live According to the Eucharist:

To move toward Eucharistic unity, we must not only debate theological positions or adjust institutional policies — we must become a **Eucharistic people**.

- People who live in continual communion with Christ.

- People who are committed to building communion with one another.

- People who carry the transforming power of God through the Eucharist into the world as ambassadors of Christ's peace.

As we move toward the conclusion of this chapter, we are reminded that the path to unity is not merely through human effort but through the divine power at work in the Eucharist itself — the sacrament through which God makes us one.

Conclusion: The Urgent Need for Eucharistic Reconciliation

The Lord's Table stands at the very center of the Christian life. It is where Christ offers Himself fully to His people, where we receive His Body and Blood, where we are joined not only to Him but to one another as one Body.

- And yet, this sacred table has become, over centuries, a point of division.

- We proclaim one Lord, but we worship at divided altars.

- We preach one baptism, but we defend separate communions.

- We call ourselves one Body, but we refuse to break bread together.

This is not the vision Christ had for His Church.

> "There is one body and one Spirit, just as also you were called in one hope of your calling; one Lord, one faith, one baptism; one God and Father of all who is over all and through all and in all" (Ephesians 4:4–6).

The urgent need of our time is not simply for better theological arguments or more ecumenical programs. The urgent need is for **a return to the heart of the Eucharist** — to recognize it as the sacrament of Christ's reconciling love, the place where His people are made one, the means by which the Church becomes the living sign of His presence in the world.

The Path Forward:

What must we do?

- **We must overcome barriers** through dialogue, love, and humility, refusing to let past wounds or current misunderstandings define the future.

- **We must call our leaders**—bishops, pastors, theologians—to take bold, prayerful steps toward healing, reconciliation, and the pursuit of visible unity.

- **We must raise our plea** as the whole people of God, longing and praying for the day when all Christians can gather again at the same altar.

- **We must live according to the Eucharist**, allowing the transforming power of the sacrament to shape our hearts, our churches, and our witness to the world.

A Time for Hope:

This is not an impossible dream. It is the very will of Christ.

The unity we seek is not something we manufacture; it is a gift that Christ Himself has already won.

The healing we long for is not beyond reach; it is the fruit of the Spirit's work in humble, faithful hearts.

The reconciliation we pray for is not a distant hope; it is the living reality of the Kingdom that is already breaking into the world.

A Final Invitation:

The Table of the Lord is set. Christ invites His people to come—not as isolated individuals, not as divided factions, but as one Body, drawn together by His love, nourished by His grace and sent out as His witnesses.

> "Blessed are those who are invited to the marriage supper of the Lamb" (Revelation 19:9).

The urgent need for Eucharistic reconciliation is nothing less than the urgent call of Christ Himself.

- Will we hear His call?

- Will we open our hearts to His healing?

- Will we take our place at His table—together?

May the Church, in every age and every place, rise to this holy calling so that the world may see, believe, and rejoice in the love of the Father, the grace of the Son, and the unity of the Holy Spirit.

Reflection: Returning Together to the Table of the Lord

As we close this chapter, we are left with a profound tension—and a profound hope.

The tension comes from the painful reality that Christ's Body remains divided at the very table meant to unite us. We carry the weight of centuries of separation, misunderstanding, and exclusion. We see the fractured witness of the Church before the world, and we grieve the absence of full Eucharistic fellowship among those who call on the same Lord.

But alongside this tension is a living hope. We believe in a God who heals wounds, breaks down dividing walls, and gathers the scattered into one. We believe in Christ who prayed—not in vain, but with the certainty of divine purpose—**"that they may all be one."** We believe in the power of God through the Eucharist, not only to nourish individuals but to restore the unity of the Church and bear witness to the reconciling love of God for all creation.

The invitation to the Lord's Table is not merely a theological idea; it is a summons to conversion, to humility, to love. It is an invitation to lay down our weapons of pride, our shields of suspicion, our walls of defensiveness—and to come together before the Lamb of God who takes away the sins of the world.

As we pray now, may we open our hearts to the work of the Spirit, who alone can lead the Church back to the unity that Christ desires for the life of the world and the glory of God.

Closing Prayer

Lord Jesus Christ,
You are the Bread of Life,
the true Vine,
the Lamb who was slain and yet lives forever.

You have set Your table before us,
inviting us to receive Your Body and Blood,
to abide in You and to be made one in You.

Yet we come before You today as a divided Church,
separated by walls of doctrine, history, and fear.
Forgive us, Lord, for the ways we have hardened our hearts,
for the times we have allowed pride or suspicion
to keep us from embracing our brothers and sisters in You.

Pour out Your Spirit upon Your people, O Lord.
Heal the wounds of division.
Guide our leaders with wisdom and courage.
Give us the humility to listen,
the grace to forgive,
and the strength to hope.

Renew in us the longing for the day.
when all who love You may gather together at one table,
sharing one Bread and one Cup,
proclaiming one faith,
and bearing one witness to the world.

Until that day comes,
make us a people who live according to the Eucharist —
offering ourselves in love,
hungering for Your presence,
and seeking always the unity for which You prayed.

We ask this in Your holy name,
You who live and reign with the Father and the Holy Spirit,
one God, forever and ever. Amen.

Chapter 11

The Marriage Supper of the Lamb

The Eucharist is not merely a remembrance of Christ's sacrifice on the cross—it is a **living participation** in God's eternal plan, a foretaste of the glory yet to come. Every time the Church gathers around the altar, it touches the edge of eternity, tasting the joy and unity that will one day be fully realized in the **Heavenly Banquet**.

> "Blessed are those who are invited to the marriage supper of the Lamb" (Revelation 19:9).

Throughout Scripture, God's purpose has always been to **gather all things into unity in Christ** (Ephesians 1:10). The scattered nations, the broken peoples, the divided hearts— God's ultimate desire is to bring them all together in one redeemed family to celebrate forever in the presence of the Lamb who was slain and who now reigns.

The Eucharist is not only a memorial of the past; it is a **window into the future**. It reveals the destiny of the Church, the fulfillment of God's promises, and the eternal joy that awaits the people of God at the final consummation of history.

What This Chapter Will Explore:

In this chapter, we will lift our eyes beyond the present divisions and struggles of the Church to contemplate the **eschatological horizon**—the future toward which the Eucharist points and for which it prepares us. We will explore:

1- **The Eucharist as a Foretaste of the Heavenly Banquet (Revelation 19:9)**

   How does each Eucharistic celebration connect us to the great wedding feast that awaits the redeemed?

2- **The Vision of the Church Gathered in Unity Before the Throne of God**

   What does Scripture reveal about the final unity of God's people, and how should that shape our efforts toward unity today?

3- **The Mission of the Church: To Prepare for the Final Consummation in Christ**

   How does the Church's mission on earth align with its future calling to gather all nations before Christ?

4- **"Until He Comes": Living Eucharistic Unity Now in Anticipation of Full Unity in the Kingdom**

   How can we embody today the unity and love we will one day share perfectly in God's eternal Kingdom?

The Challenge of Living the Future Now:

- If the Eucharist is truly a preparation for eternity, how can we continue to approach it in a spirit of division and separation?

- How can we participate in the one Bread and one Cup while remaining fractured in heart and community?

- How can we proclaim the unity of the coming Kingdom while defending divided altars and excluding one another from the table?

This chapter is a call to the Church to **live its future reality in the present**—to align its practices, its hopes, and its relationships with the final unity that Christ has already won and will one day fully reveal.

We are not only waiting for the Kingdom; we are called to anticipate it, embody it, and proclaim it now, especially through the Eucharist.

- **The Eucharist is the foretaste of the final feast.**

- **The Eucharist is the pledge of the Church's eternal unity.**

- **The Eucharist is the call to live today as we will live forever: one people, one Body, one Bride before the Lamb.**

As we enter this chapter, may we open our hearts to the eschatological hope of the Church, allowing the Eucharist to reshape not only our vision of the future but also our commitment to love and unity here and now.

1. The Eucharist as a Foretaste of the Heavenly Banquet (Revelation 19:9)

At the heart of the Christian faith is a promise: that history is moving toward a glorious consummation when all things will be gathered up and perfected in Christ. This is not an abstract or distant dream—it is the living hope that shapes our present, nourishes our faith, and directs the Church's mission.

Nowhere is this future hope more beautifully portrayed than in the image of the **Heavenly Banquet**, the wedding feast of the Lamb described in the Book of Revelation:

> "Blessed are those who are invited to the marriage supper [the wedding feast] of the Lamb" (Revelation 19:9).

This is the end toward which all creation is moving: a cosmic celebration, a joyful gathering of the redeemed, a wedding feast where Christ, the Bridegroom, is united with His Church, the Bride, in perfect and eternal communion.

The Eucharist as a Present Participation in Future Glory:

The Eucharist is not merely a symbolic remembrance of what Christ has done; it is a **real participation** in what Christ is doing—and will ultimately complete.

Just as Israel ate the Passover meal, not merely to remember the past but to anticipate future deliverance, so the Church partakes of the Eucharist in anticipation of the final redemption.

The Eucharist is not simply an earthly rite; it is a heavenly mystery. In every Eucharistic celebration, the Church is drawn up into the eternal worship of heaven, joining the angels and saints in the praise of the Lamb.

As we eat the Bread of Life and drink the Cup of Salvation, we receive a foretaste of the eternal feast, a preview of the unending joy that awaits the faithful in the Kingdom of God.

This is why the Eucharist has always been called **the pledge of eternal life** — because, in it, Christ gives Himself as the food that nourishes us now and prepares us for everlasting communion with Him.

The Witness of the Early Church:

The early Church understood the Eucharist not only as a present gift but as a future promise. **St. Ignatius of Antioch**, writing in the second century, called the Eucharist:

> "The medicine of immortality, the antidote against death, that we should live forever in Christ" (*Letter to the Ephesians* 20).

For Ignatius and the early martyrs, the Eucharist was not just a comfort in times of trial; it was the assurance that death itself had been conquered, that eternal life was already breaking into the present, and that the Church's destiny was secure in Christ.

The Eucharist and the Wedding Feast of the Lamb:

The Book of Revelation reveals that the ultimate destiny of the Church is to be united with Christ at the great wedding feast of the Lamb. This eschatological vision gives profound meaning to every Eucharistic celebration:

- Each time the Church gathers at the altar, it is rehearsing for the final banquet, practicing the eternal song of praise, and anticipating the moment when faith will give way to sight.

- The Eucharist is a living link between heaven and earth, a sacred participation in the mystery of the Kingdom that is both already here and not yet fully realized.

Every time we receive the Body and Blood of Christ, we are reminded: **this is what you were made for**—eternal communion, perfect joy, unbroken fellowship with God and with all His saints.

A Challenge to Our Divisions:

If the Eucharist is truly our foretaste of eternal unity, how can we continue to celebrate it in a spirit of division? How can we come to the altar expecting to join the heavenly feast while refusing to be reconciled with our brothers and sisters on earth?

St. Paul's warning to the Corinthians remains urgent for us today:

> "For he who eats and drinks, eats and drinks judgment to himself if he does not judge the body rightly [discern the Body rightly]" (1 Corinthians 11:29).

To discern the Body of Christ is not only to recognize His presence in the sacrament but also to recognize His presence in His people. Eucharistic unity is not an optional bonus; it is a requirement of true communion.

Reflection:

- Do we approach the Eucharist as a mere ritual or as a living anticipation of the heavenly banquet?

- How might our divisions at the altar distort the vision of unity that God intends for His people?

- Are we allowing the Eucharist to shape not only our personal piety but also our communal identity as one Body in Christ?

A Call to Anticipate Heaven Now:

The Eucharist invites the Church to live in the present with eyes fixed on the future. Every time we gather to break bread, we are declaring: **The Kingdom is coming. The Bridegroom is returning. The feast is being prepared.**

May we approach the Lord's Table with hearts ready to embrace not only Christ but all who belong to Him, knowing that we are being prepared for the day when we will all sit down together at the wedding feast of the Lamb, rejoicing in perfect unity and eternal love.

2. The Vision of the Church Gathered in Unity Before the Throne of God

From the very beginning, the Church has carried within her heart a vision — a vision not just of her life on earth but of her destiny in heaven, where all believers will be gathered together in perfect communion before the throne of God. This vision is vividly portrayed in the Book of Revelation, where John describes the great multitude of the redeemed:

> "After these things, I looked, and behold, a great multitude which no one could count, from every nation and all tribes and peoples and tongues, standing before the throne and before the Lamb, clothed in white robes, and palm branches were in their hands; and they cry out with a loud voice, saying, 'Salvation belongs to our God who sits on the throne and to the Lamb!'" (Revelation 7:9-10).

This is the Church as she is meant to be — gathered from every corner of the earth, from every race, tribe, and language, standing as one before the Lamb of God, offering praise with a single voice. In this heavenly vision, we see no trace of division, no denominational boundaries, no historical schisms. There are no Catholic or Orthodox sections, no Protestant or Evangelical rows, and no ancient or modern distinctions. There is only the one redeemed people of God, clothed in the white robes of salvation, united in the joy of eternal worship.

It is this destiny that gives the Church her deepest identity. We are not merely a collection of communities scattered across the earth; we are a people on a pilgrimage toward a common home. We are citizens of heaven (Philippians 3:20), and our present life is shaped by the hope of the future glory to which we are called.

The Present Shapes the Future — and the Future Shapes the Present

What does it mean for the Church to know that her final destiny is unity before the throne of God? It means that every act of division, every defense of separation, and every refusal to reconcile stands in painful contrast to the unity we proclaim as our eternal hope. If heaven holds a place for all who belong to Christ, how can we justify excluding one another from the altar here on earth?

St. Augustine, reflecting on the nature of the Church, reminds us that our divisions are alien to the eternal banquet that awaits us:

> "In heaven, there are no separate tables for different peoples. There is one feast, one banquet, one Christ for all" (Sermon 227).

When we come to the Eucharistic table, we are participating not only in an earthly rite but in a heavenly reality. We are joining, by anticipation, the worship of the angels and saints, the unending praise that fills the courts of heaven. How then, can we come to that table divided? How can we profess one Body, one Spirit, one hope, one Lord (Ephesians 4:4–5) — yet approach separate altars, refusing to break bread with one another?

The Tragedy of Divided Worship:

The truth is that the divisions among Christians are not only theological or historical wounds; they are wounds in the visible body of Christ on earth, and they cast a shadow over the witness of the Gospel to the world. Jesus prayed, **"that they may all be one... so that the world may believe that You sent Me"** (John 17:21). When the world looks upon a Church fragmented by centuries of dispute, how can it see the reflection of Christ's love?

Every Eucharistic celebration is meant to be a sign of unity, a foretaste of the wedding feast of the Lamb. But when Christians celebrate the Eucharist apart from one another, when they withhold communion, when they deny the shared nature of the Lord's Table, they send a message of brokenness rather than reconciliation.

This is not to ignore the real theological issues that remain between traditions nor to suggest that unity can be achieved by ignoring truth. But it is to say that the ultimate truth is the truth of God's reconciling love and that the divisions we now tolerate must be judged in light of the unity that God Himself promises and will one day bring to fulfillment.

A Vision That Demands a Response:

The vision of the heavenly Church gathered before the throne is not a passive promise; it is a summons. It calls the Church on earth to begin now what she will one day experience in fullness. It calls her to live in the present in a way that reflects her future destiny.

We cannot claim to long for the unity of heaven while remaining content with the divisions of earth. We cannot pray, "Your Kingdom come, Your will be done, on earth as it is in heaven," while refusing to take even small steps toward the reconciliation that will define our eternal life together.

This heavenly vision also gives the Church courage. If we know that unity is God's ultimate will, we can work for it with hope, trusting that we are aligning ourselves with His eternal purpose. We can persevere in dialogue, in prayer, in acts of shared witness and service, confident that the Spirit is already at work leading the Church into the unity that reflects the very nature of God.

Reflection:

As we contemplate this vision, we are invited to ask ourselves hard but essential questions:

- Do we allow the promise of heavenly unity to shape the way we live our faith here and now?

- Are we willing to lay aside pride, suspicion, or fear to move toward our brothers and sisters in Christ, knowing that we are destined to stand together before God's throne?

- How might our Eucharistic celebrations today begin to mirror the undivided worship of the saints in heaven?

The future is not only a hope; it is a calling. The vision of the Church gathered in unity before the throne of God is meant to transform us now, calling us out of our divisions and into the communion for which Christ died.

As we move forward, we will explore how the Church's mission on earth — to proclaim the Gospel and prepare the world for Christ's return — is intimately tied to this eschatological vision. Through the Eucharist, God does not only point us forward; He equips and sends us to live as witnesses of the unity that Christ has already won and will one day bring to glorious completion.

3. The Mission of the Church: To Prepare for the Final Consummation in Christ

The Church does not exist merely to maintain religious traditions or preserve sacred spaces. The Church exists because

God has called her into being as His instrument of redemption, reconciliation, and transformation in the world. She is not only the community of the redeemed; she is also the living sign and active agent of God's saving plan.

At the heart of the Church's mission is a clear and urgent purpose: **to prepare for the final consummation in Christ**, when all things will be gathered into Him, healed, and made whole.

> "Making known to us the mystery of His will, according to His good pleasure which He purposed in Him for an administration of the fullness of the times, that is, the summing up of all things in Christ, things in the heavens and things on the earth in Him" (Ephesians 1:9–10).

This mission is not vague or abstract; it takes on concrete form in the life, worship, and sacramental practice of the Church. Above all, it is focused and embodied in the Eucharist — the sacrament where the past, present, and future converge, where the Church both anticipates and proclaims the coming Kingdom.

The Eucharist as the Heart of the Church's Mission:

The Eucharist is not only the source and summit of the Church's life; it is the driving force behind her mission. Every time the Church gathers at the Lord's Table, she is drawn deeper into her identity and sent forth to fulfill her calling.

In the Eucharist, the Church proclaims the Gospel, announcing the saving death and resurrection of Christ.

In the Eucharist, the Church enacts reconciliation, gathering believers into one Body and breaking down barriers of division, suspicion, and exclusion.

In the Eucharist, the Church is sanctified, nourished by the very life of Christ and prepared for the glory of the Kingdom.

St. Paul captures this dynamic beautifully:

> "For as often as you eat this bread and drink the cup, you proclaim the death of the Lord until He comes" (1 Corinthians 11:26).

In every Eucharistic celebration, the Church is both looking backward to the cross and forward to the return of Christ, proclaiming the mystery of faith and preparing the world for its final consummation.

The Call to Evangelization and Reconciliation:

The mission of the Church is fundamentally Eucharistic — but this does not mean it is confined to the sanctuary. On the contrary, through the Eucharist, God equips the Church to go out into the world, bearing witness to Christ and extending His reconciling love.

The Church is called to **evangelize**, inviting all people to share in the communion of Christ's Body and Blood.

The Church is called to **reconcile**, healing divisions not only among Christians but within the human family, embodying the peace that Christ has accomplished on the cross.

The Church is called to **sanctify**, transforming individuals and communities by the grace of the sacraments and the power of the Holy Spirit.

In this sense, the Eucharist is both a **gift** and a **mission**: through it, God feeds the Church, and He sends the Church.

The Urgency of Preparing for Christ's Return:

The Church does not simply wait passively for the end of time; she actively prepares for it, longing for the return of her Lord and working to bring as many as possible into the joy of the Kingdom. The Eucharist keeps this eschatological urgency alive.

Every time we receive the Body and Blood of Christ, we are reminded that **He is coming again** — and that we are to live in a way worthy of His coming.

Every act of Eucharistic sharing, every step toward reconciliation, is a sign that the Church is not content with division but is preparing herself as a Bride adorned for her Husband (Revelation 21:2).

Every Eucharistic celebration is a rehearsal for the final wedding feast of the Lamb, where God's people will rejoice in eternal communion.

St. John Chrysostom challenges us:

> "How can you approach the same table and yet remain divided? This table is not a table of separation, but of reconciliation" (*Homily on 1 Corinthians* 24:4).

If we are serious about preparing for Christ's return, then Eucharistic unity cannot be treated as a secondary or optional matter. It is central to the Church's witness and mission.

Reflection:

- Are we, as a Church, allowing the Eucharist to shape and propel our mission to the world?

- How can we better embody the reconciling, sanctifying power of the Eucharist in our relationships, communities, and outreach?

- What practical steps can the Church take to ensure that its mission aligns with the unity and hope of the coming Kingdom?

A Church on Mission Toward the Kingdom:

The mission of the Church is not only to preserve the past or endure the present — it is to prepare for the glorious future that God has promised. The Eucharist is at the heart of this mission: a gift that draws us into Christ, a challenge that calls us to live as His Body, and a foretaste that fills us with longing for the day when all things will be made new.

As we move into the next section, we will reflect on how the Church is called to **live now** in anticipation of that final unity — not merely hoping for it in the future but embodying it in the present "until He comes."

4. "Until He Comes": Living Eucharistic Unity Now in Anticipation of Full Unity in the Kingdom

The Eucharist holds the Church suspended between time and eternity. Each celebration is an act of memory, recalling Christ's death and resurrection, but it is also an act of hope, longing for the day when He will return, and all things will be made new. St. Paul's words remind us of this profound tension:

> "For as often as you eat this bread and drink the cup, you proclaim the death of the Lord until He comes" (1 Corinthians 11:26).

In these simple words — "until He comes" — the Church finds her mission, her calling, and her hope. She is a people who live not only by looking backward to what Christ has done but by looking forward to what Christ will do. The Eucharist is not just a sacred routine; it is the living pulse of the Church's eschatological hope, a moment when the future breaks into the present, and we are given a taste of the glory yet to come.

Living as a People of Anticipation:

To live in the light of the coming Kingdom is to live in anticipation. But this anticipation is not passive, not simply a matter of waiting. It is active, shaping the Church's life, its relationships, and its mission.

The early Christians understood this well. They did not gather around the Eucharistic table merely as a closed circle remembering past events; they gathered as a people preparing for a wedding banquet, adorning themselves with the virtues of love, humility, forgiveness, and reconciliation. Every Eucharistic celebration was a rehearsal for eternity — a time when they aligned their lives with the reality of Christ's reign.

The Eucharist was the space where they practiced heaven: where social divisions were overcome, where Jew and Gentile, rich and poor, male and female, slave and free, became one Body in Christ. They knew that the table of the Lord was a foretaste of the heavenly banquet, and they sought to live accordingly — not passively waiting for God to impose unity but actively working to embody it here and now.

The Ongoing Invitation to Unity:

At the Eucharistic table, Christ's invitation to unity is constant, ongoing, and urgent. It is not something He withholds until we achieve perfect theological agreement; it is something He offers now so that through sharing His Body and Blood, we might be drawn into deeper communion.

The Eucharist is not merely the reward of the reconciled; it is the very act of reconciliation itself. Each time we come forward to receive the Bread of Life, we are proclaiming not only our love for Christ but our belonging to His Body — and that Body includes all those whom He has redeemed by His blood across time, space, and denomination.

This is why division at the Eucharistic table is such a profound contradiction. To kneel before the Lamb who gave Himself for the unity of His people while simultaneously refusing to be reconciled with one's brothers and sisters is to deny the very meaning of the sacrament. The Eucharist calls us to a life shaped by forgiveness, generosity, and open-heartedness, not by suspicion or exclusion.

A Witness for the World:

The unity of the Church is not only an internal matter; it is part of her witness to the world. When Jesus prayed, **"that they may all be one… so that the world may believe that You sent Me"** (John 17:21), He revealed the missionary dimension of Christian unity. The credibility of the Gospel is at stake in how the Church embodies her unity. A divided Church proclaims a divided Christ; a reconciled Church proclaims the reconciling power of God.

Eucharistic unity, therefore, is not a secondary concern; it is central to the Church's vocation. It is not a private devotional issue; it is part of her public proclamation of the Kingdom. If we truly long for Christ's return, we must ask ourselves whether we are living in a way that reflects the unity He prayed for, the unity He died for, and the unity He will one day bring to perfect fulfillment.

Becoming What We Receive:

In the Eucharist, the Church becomes what she receives. As St. Augustine famously taught:

> "Behold what you are; become what you receive — the Body of Christ" (*Sermon 272*).

To receive the Body of Christ in the Eucharist is to be called into the life of the Body of Christ in the world. We cannot receive Him truly without being drawn into communion with one another. We cannot approach the altar without also approaching one another in love.

This means that Eucharistic unity is not only a theological or institutional goal; it is a personal and communal vocation. It calls every believer to examine the heart:

- Am I living in a spirit of reconciliation and forgiveness?

- Am I willing to lay down my pride and open my heart to fellow Christians, even those from different traditions?

- Am I allowing the Eucharist to shape not only my relationship with God but also my relationships within the Church?

Living the Future Now:

The phrase "until He comes" is a summons to live the future now. We are not called to wait for unity to fall from heaven passively; we are called to begin living that unity now, trusting that the Holy Spirit will complete what we begin in faith.

- Every small step toward reconciliation is an anticipation of the Kingdom.

- Every act of shared prayer, shared service, and shared love is a sign of the world to come.

- Every effort to break down barriers at the Eucharistic table is a witness to the hope that we will one day gather, all together, at the great wedding feast of the Lamb.

A Eucharistic People on the Journey:

To live as a Eucharistic people is to live as a people on the way — a people who know where they are going and who shape their lives accordingly. We are not wandering aimlessly; we are journeying toward the day when God will be all in all, when the Bride of Christ will stand before Him in splendor, without spot or wrinkle, holy and blameless (Ephesians 5:27). The Eucharist is both the nourishment for this journey and the pattern of the destination. It is the place where heaven touches the earth and where we are invited to live now in the unity we will one day share fully.

Let us not delay. Let us not settle for half-measures or remain content with our divisions. Let us live, even now, as one Body, one Spirit, one hope, because we know that the day is coming when Christ will return, and we will be gathered at His table forever.

Conclusion: The Urgent Call to Eucharistic Reconciliation

As we come to the end of this chapter, we stand at the intersection of time and eternity. The Eucharist reveals to us the full scope of God's redemptive plan: a plan that reaches from the cross and the empty tomb all the way to the heavenly throne, where the redeemed of every age and nation will gather in perfect unity and joy.

This is the vision that gives meaning and direction to the Church's life on earth. We are not merely a scattered collection of congregations or denominations clinging to survival or defending tradition; we are the pilgrim Bride of Christ, moving with longing and hope toward the great wedding feast of the Lamb.

But if that is true, then we must ask hard and urgent questions:

- How can we claim to long for the unity of heaven while we cling to the divisions of earth?

- How can we proclaim the love and reconciliation of Christ while we remain estranged from one another at His table?

- How can we prepare for the coming Kingdom if we are unwilling to live now in the unity that will one day define us?

The Eucharist calls the Church to **become what she receives**: the one Body of Christ, broken yet whole, wounded yet healed, scattered yet gathered into perfect communion. The call to Eucharistic reconciliation is not a peripheral issue; it is central to the identity, mission, and future of the Church.

We live in the "until He comes" time — a time of anticipation, preparation, and hope. Let us live it well. Let us begin even now to embody the unity, holiness, and joy we will one day share in fullness so that when the Lord returns, He will find His Bride ready, adorned in love, and gathered as one.

Reflection: Preparing Our Hearts for the Feast

Pause for a moment and imagine it:

- The great banquet table is set in heaven.

- The Bridegroom, Christ Himself, welcoming His people.
- The countless multitude — from every tribe, tongue, and nation — clothed in white robes, waving palm branches, singing songs of salvation before the Lamb.

This is your destiny. This is the Church's destiny. This is what the Eucharist points to, week after week, drawing you forward with every step.

But this destiny is not just about someday; it is about now.

- Are you living as someone preparing for the feast?
- Are you nurturing a heart of unity, forgiveness, and love?
- Are you allowing the grace of God through the Eucharist to shape how you view fellow Christians, even those from traditions or communities different from your own?

The call is not only to look forward but to live forward — to embody today the unity and holiness that will one day be perfected in Christ.

The time is now. The invitation is open. The Eucharist awaits.

Closing Prayer

Eternal Father,
You have called us by Your grace,
into the Body of Your beloved Son,

and You have set before us the banquet of life,
the table of Your Kingdom,
where heaven and earth meet,
where Christ offers Himself for the life of the world.

We come before You today with hearts longing for unity,
grieving the divisions that have wounded Your Church,
confessing the pride and fear that keep us apart,
and asking for the healing power of Your Spirit.

Make us one, O Lord, as You are one.
Draw us together by Your power through the Eucharist,
that we may become what we receive —
the Body of Christ, broken and poured out for the world.

Prepare us for the day when Christ will return in glory,
when the Bride will stand before the Bridegroom,
when the wedding feast of the Lamb will be fulfilled,
and all creation will rejoice in Your eternal love.

Until that day, help us to live as faithful witnesses,
offering our lives in service,
opening our hearts in reconciliation,
and proclaiming with joy the mystery of faith:
Christ has died, Christ is risen, Christ will come again.

We ask this through Jesus Christ our Lord,
who lives and reigns with You and the Holy Spirit,
one God, now and forever. Amen.

Conclusion

The Eucharist as the Heart of the Christian Unity

As we arrive at the end of this journey, we are brought back to the center: the Eucharist — not merely as a sacrament or a ritual, but as the beating heart of Christian life and unity.

From the earliest days of the Church, believers gathered at one table, breaking bread with joy and simplicity of heart, united by their love for Christ and for one another. In the Acts of the Apostles, we read how they "were continually devoting themselves to the apostles' teaching and to the fellowship, to the breaking of bread and to the prayers" (Acts 2:42). This image of the early Church is not only a picture of historical faithfulness but a challenge and summons to the Church today.

Over the centuries, however, the unity Christ so passionately prayed for — **"that they may all be one"** (John 17:21) — has been fractured. What was once a single table has become many, divided by walls of doctrine, tradition, history, and, at times, human pride and misunderstanding. The very meal that was given to unite has often become a sign of separation.

This book has sought to trace the biblical, theological, and historical meaning of the Eucharist and to lift up its profound role as the heart of Christian unity. But more than that, it has sought to issue a challenge — a call to action — because unity is not merely something we can admire from afar or study as an academic subject. It is something we are called to embody, to live, and to make visible in the world.

Recap of the Journey We Have Taken:

We began by exploring the deep roots of the Eucharist in the Old Testament, seeing how the Passover, the manna in the wilderness, and the covenantal meals pointed forward to Christ's gift of His Body and Blood. We reflected on the Last Supper, where Christ instituted the New Covenant and entrusted to His Church the perpetual memorial of His sacrifice.

We examined how the Eucharist, from the earliest centuries, was understood as the sacrament of unity — the place where believers became one Body in Christ, where distinctions of race, class, and background were dissolved in the presence of the crucified and risen Lord.

And yet we also faced the painful reality of how the Eucharist has become, over time, a source of division — not because Christ has changed, but because His followers have fractured. We explored the historical schisms, doctrinal disagreements, and ecclesiastical decisions that have contributed to the divided state of Christendom, asking: is it possible to reverse this trend? Is it possible to reclaim the Eucharist as the bond of love it was always meant to be?

We looked forward to the heavenly banquet, the eschatological feast where all the redeemed will gather before the Lamb. We reminded ourselves that in heaven, there will be no Catholic or Protestant, no East or West, no ancient or modern — only the one Bride gathered to her Bridegroom, rejoicing in eternal communion. And if that is our destiny, we must ask how we can begin to live it even now.

Moving from Words to Action:

Unity is not something that happens automatically or by accident. It requires courage, humility, repentance, and intentional effort. It requires us to move beyond theoretical aspirations or polite gestures and into concrete, lived expressions of communion.

Jesus did not command us to love one another **when we had solved all theological disagreements**; He commanded us to love one another as the defining mark of discipleship (John 13:35). And He gave us the Eucharist — His own Body and Blood — as the means by which that love is nourished, deepened, and made visible.

We must now ask ourselves:

- How can we continue to guard the Eucharist as a treasure of separation rather than a gift of reconciliation?

- How can we claim to be the Body of Christ while refusing to break bread with fellow believers?

- How can we preach the hope of the Kingdom while passively waiting for unity to come in heaven without doing the work of love and reconciliation here on earth?

The world is watching. A divided Church weakens the credibility of the Gospel. A Church that is united at the Lord's Table, despite differences, bears radiant witness to the power of Christ's love to reconcile all things.

An Invitation to the Final Steps:

This concluding chapter offers not only a summary but an invitation. It invites every reader, every believer, every community, and every leader to take practical steps toward restoring Eucharistic unity — not by abandoning truth, but by allowing truth to lead us into deeper love.

It invites us to reconsider how we treat the Lord's Table:

- Is it a wall or a bridge?

- Is it a prize for the perfected or a means of grace for sinners?

- Is it a private possession or a public sign of Christ's reconciling love?

The Eucharist is where the Church becomes what she is meant to be: one Body in Christ, broken yet whole, many yet one, wounded yet healed. The time has come to move from division to communion, from exclusion to embrace, from speaking about unity to living it visibly, powerfully, and sacramentally.

The Lord's Table is set. The invitation is open. Will we come together? Will we answer the call?

Practical Steps Toward Eucharistic Sharing

The Eucharist as the Heart of Christian Unity:

We now reach the end of this journey — but in truth, it is not an ending, but a beginning.

Throughout this book, we have followed the path of the Eucharist from its biblical roots, through its theological depths, across the centuries of Church history, and into its eschatological promise. We have seen how the Eucharist stands as both the center and the summit of Christian life: the place where Christ gives Himself to His people, the mystery where heaven and earth meet, and the sacrament that reveals and creates the unity of the Church.

Yet we have also confronted the painful paradox: the Eucharist, which was given as the sign and source of unity, has too often become the very place where divisions are most visible. Instead of gathering around one table, we approach many; instead of sharing one Bread, we cling to separate altars; instead of embracing one another as brothers and sisters in Christ, we let doctrinal disputes, historical wounds, and ecclesial boundaries keep us apart.

This book has been a meditation, a lament, and most of all, a call — a call to action.

It is no longer enough to admire the idea of unity or to speak of it in lofty theological terms. **Unity must be lived.** It must be made visible in the Church's daily life, in her Eucharistic celebrations, in the way believers love one another across boundaries, and in the way we testify to the world that Christ's love has the power to reconcile all things.

Beyond Words: A Call to Action

Christ's invitation is clear. He calls us not to a theoretical unity that waits for perfection but to a lived unity that begins now — humble, imperfect, fragile, but real.

To take up this call will require courage.

- Courage to face our differences honestly, without minimizing them or sweeping them aside.

- Courage to listen with respect, to enter into dialogue, to recognize the work of the Spirit in traditions not our own.

- Courage to set aside pride and suspicion, to open our hearts, and to let love lead us forward.

It will also require humility.

- Humility to acknowledge the sins of the past and the wounds they have caused.

- Humility to admit that none of us possesses the fullness of truth in isolation.

- Humility to recognize that the Eucharist is not a prize we control but a gift we receive — a gift meant for the whole Body of Christ.

Finally, it will require hope.

- Hope that Christ's prayer for unity will be fulfilled.

- Hope that the Spirit is already at work, often in hidden ways, bringing the Church toward reconciliation.

- Hope that as we gather at the Eucharistic table, we are participating not only in a present reality but in a future promise — the foretaste of the heavenly banquet where all God's people will rejoice as one.

Living Eucharistic Unity: Practical Invitations

What might this look like in our daily lives and communities?

First, it begins with the heart.

Before we can approach the table together, we must open our hearts to one another, allowing the Spirit to heal old prejudices, soften rigid attitudes, and awaken new compassion.

- Are we willing to see Christ in those we have regarded as "other"?

- Are we willing to pray for unity, not as a vague ideal, but as a personal longing?

Second, it requires shared encounters.

Where possible, Christians from different traditions should pray together, study Scripture together, serve together, and build friendships that transcend ecclesial labels. Common worship, ecumenical gatherings, and acts of shared mission allow us to experience one another not as rivals but as fellow members of Christ's Body.

Third, it calls for pastoral sensitivity and theological courage.

Church leaders have a sacred duty to guide their flocks toward unity — not by compromising truth, but by seeking ways to foster greater Eucharistic hospitality, recognizing the deep bonds of baptism and faith that already unite us. Could moments of Eucharistic sharing, carefully discerned and pastorally guided, become signs of hope and steps toward fuller reconciliation?

Finally, it requires us to live in anticipation of the Kingdom.

The Eucharist is the place where the future breaks into the present. Every time we receive the Body and Blood of Christ, we are rehearsing for the day when we will all gather at the heavenly banquet. Why wait until eternity to live the unity that God has already promised?

A Final Prayer for the Unity of Christ's Body

Let us lift our hearts now in prayer, entrusting ourselves, our churches, and the entire Body of Christ to the God who makes all things new:

Lord Jesus Christ, Bread of Life,
You gave Yourself to us on the night You were betrayed,
and You continue to give Yourself to Your Church,
that we may live in You and be one in You.

You prayed for unity,
You suffered for unity,
You died and rose again to reconcile all things to Yourself.

Yet we have divided Your Body, Lord.
We have built walls around Your table,
and we have let fear, pride, and misunderstanding keep us apart.

Have mercy on us.
Forgive us.
Heal us.
Break down the barriers we have built.

Send Your Holy Spirit upon Your Church,
to open minds, renew hearts, and guide our steps.
Give wisdom to our leaders,
courage to our communities,
and love to all who seek You.

Make us one, Lord, as You and the Father are one,
so that the world may believe,
and so that we may one day gather as one people,
around one table,
sharing one Bread and one Cup,
in the joy of Your eternal Kingdom.

Until that day,
teach us to live as Your Body in the world,
to love as You have loved,
and to walk the path of unity with hope and faith,
knowing that You who have begun this work
will bring it to completion
on the day of Your glorious return.

For You live and reign with the Father and the Holy Spirit,
one God, forever and ever. Amen.

The Table Is Set — The Invitation Is Given

The time for waiting is over. The invitation has been given. Christ Himself stands at the head of the table, His hands extended, His heart open.

The Eucharist is not ours to control; it is His gift, His presence, His love poured out for the life of the world.

Let us no longer delay. Let us no longer be content with divided tables. Let us take the first steps — however small, however trembling — toward the unity for which Christ died and rose again.

> "T*here is* one body and one Spirit, just as also you were called in one hope of your calling; one Lord, one faith, one baptism; one God and Father of all who is over all and through all and in all" (Ephesians 4:4–6).

And the day will come when we will all gather as one, at the wedding feast of the Lamb, where every tear will be wiped away, and love will reign forever.

Until that day, let us live, love, and walk in hope. The Table is set. The invitation stands. Let us come — together.

Epilogue

A Personal Word from the Author

As I bring this book to a close, I find myself not at the end of a project but at the threshold of a lifelong prayer.

This work has been written not as a detached theological exercise but as the labor of a heart burdened by love for the Church. This heart longs to see the day when Christ's followers will stand together, side by side, at one altar, lifting up one voice, sharing one Bread and one Cup, proclaiming with one heart the glorious mystery of faith.

I have written these pages knowing full well the weight of history, the complexity of doctrine, and the real challenges that face the Church in seeking Eucharistic unity. But I have also written them with the unshakable conviction that **unity is not only possible — it is the will of Christ**. It is His prayer, His desire, and His gift to His people.

The divisions among Christians did not begin overnight, and they will not be healed overnight. But I believe — with all my heart — that every act of love, every step toward understanding, every effort to pray together and serve together, every decision to prioritize Christ over our inherited boundaries is part of the Spirit's work of healing the Body of Christ.

This book has been my small offering, a voice among many calling the Church back to the heart of her identity: to the table where Christ gives Himself, where we are made one, where heaven and earth meet, where the Kingdom is already breaking into the present.

A Personal Invitation

If you have walked through these pages with me, I invite you now to do more than close the cover and move on. I invite you to carry this prayer into your heart, into your community, into your daily walk of faith.

Pray for unity. Work for reconciliation. Reach out in love across the boundaries that divide. Support efforts at dialogue and shared witness. And most of all, let the Eucharist shape your life — making you one with Christ and through Him, one with all His people.

We may not see the fullness of Eucharistic unity in our lifetime. But every step matters. Every act of love is a seed planted. Every moment of hope is a signpost pointing toward the day when Christ will make all things new.

I pray that you, dear reader, will be part of that work — that you will be an instrument of peace, a bearer of reconciliation, and a living witness to the unity that Christ desires for His Church.

With Gratitude

To every reader, every seeker, every pilgrim on the journey of faith: thank you for walking this road with me. May the Lord bless you and keep you. May He make His face shine upon you and be gracious to you. May He lift up His countenance upon you and give you peace — the peace of unity, the peace of His love, the peace that surpasses all understanding.

Together, let us long for the day when we will gather as one Body at the wedding feast of the Lamb to rejoice forever in the presence of the One who gave Himself for us all.

Until that day — let us come to the Table, and let us come together.

In Christ's love,

Hegumen Abraam Sleman

Bibliography

Augustine of Hippo. *Sermons on the New Testament Lessons*. New City Press, 1993.

Augustine of Hippo. *Sermons on Selected Lessons of the New Testament*. New City Press, 1995.

Bradshaw, Paul F. *The Eucharistic Liturgies: Their Evolution and Interpretation*. SPCK Publishing, 2004.

Daley, Brian E. *The Hope of the Early Church: A Handbook of Patristic Eschatology*. Cambridge University Press, 1991.

Ignatius of Antioch. *Letters*. In *The Apostolic Fathers*, translated by Bart D. Ehrman, Harvard University Press, 2003.

Johnson, Maxwell E. *The Rites of Christian Initiation: Their Evolution and Interpretation*. Liturgical Press, 2007.

Jungmann, Josef A. *The Early Liturgy: To the Time of Gregory the Great*. University of Notre Dame Press, 1959.

McPartlan, Paul. *The Eucharist Makes the Church: Henri de Lubac and John Zizioulas in Dialogue*. T&T Clark, 1993.

Pelikan, Jaroslav. *The Christian Tradition: A History of the Development of Doctrine, Vol. 1*. University of Chicago Press, 1971.

Schmemann, Alexander. *The Eucharist: Sacrament of the Kingdom*. St. Vladimir's Seminary Press, 1987.

St. Basil the Great. *On the Holy Spirit*. St. Vladimir's Seminary Press, 1980.

St. Cyril of Alexandria. *Commentary on the Gospel of John*. Catholic University of America Press, 2000.

St. Irenaeus of Lyons. *Against Heresies*. Paulist Press, 1992.

St. John Chrysostom. *Homilies on the Gospel of John*. Catholic University of America Press, 2002.

Tillard, J.-M. R. *Church of Churches: The Ecclesiology of Communion*. Liturgical Press, 1992.

Zizioulas, John D. *Being as Communion: Studies in Personhood and the Church*. St. Vladimir's Seminary Press, 1985.

Back Cover Text

The Eucharist stands at the heart of Christian faith as the living presence of Christ and the visible expression of the Church's unity. Yet the sacrament meant to gather the faithful into one Body has too often become a sign of division.

In "The Eucharist: Heart of the Christian Unity," Hegumen Abraam Sleman offers a biblical and theological reflection on the Eucharist as the gracious work of the Father, who gathers His children together in Christ. Drawing from Holy Scripture, the witness of the early Church, and the sacramental life of Christianity, this book explores how Eucharistic communion reveals the Church's true identity and calls her to live the unity she proclaims.

Written in a reverent and ecumenical spirit, this work invites all who love the Eucharist to rediscover it as the heart of the Christian life—and the path toward the true unity in Christ at the Lord's Table.

www.ingramcontent.com/pod-product-compliance
Lightning Source LLC
Chambersburg PA
CBHW071153160426
43196CB00011B/2072